TRIED & TRANSFIGURED

Tried & Transfigured

Leonard Ravenhill

BETHANY HOUSE PUBLISHERS
MINNEAPOLIS, MINNESOTA 55438
A Division of Bethany Fellowship, Inc.

Fifth printing, 1982

Tried and Transfigured
Leonard Ravenhill

Library of Congress Catalog Card Number 81-71752

ISBN 0-87123-544-7

Published by Bethany House Publishers
6820 Auto Club Road, Minneapolis, Minnesota 55438

Printed in the United States of America

To

my

esteemed friend,

Norman P. Grubb,

Hon. International Secretary

of

the Worldwide

Evangelization Crusade,

whose

first book

FENTON HALL

first

caused me to feel

an

obligation

to

lost men—

this book

is

affectionately dedicated

LEONARD RAVENHILL was born in 1907 in the city of Leeds, in Yorkshire, England. After his conversion to Christ, he was trained for the ministry at Cliff College. It soon became evident that evangelism was his forté and he engaged in it with both vigor and power. Eventually he became one of England's foremost outdoor evangelists. His meetings in the war years drew traffic-jamming crowds in Britain, and great numbers of his converts not only followed the Saviour into the Kingdom, but into the Christian ministry and the world's mission fields. In 1939, he married an Irish nurse, and from that union have come three sons. Paul and David are themselves ministers of the gospel, and Phillip is a teacher. Leonard and his wife now live near Lindale, Texas, from which place Ravenhill travels to widely scattered preaching points in conference ministry.

Other books by Ravenhill

Why Revival Tarries
Meat for Men
Sodom Had No Bible
America Is Too Young to Die
Revival Praying
A Treasury of Prayer
(compiled and condensed from E. M. Bounds' works)

ACKNOWLEDGMENTS

From *The New Testament in Modern English*, © J. B. Phillips 1958. Used by permission of The Macmillan Company, New York 11, N.Y.

From *The New Testament in Modern English*, © J. B. Phillips 1958. Used by permission of G. Bles, Ltd., 52 Doughty Street, London, W.C. 1, England.

From *He Sent Leanness*, by David Head, © Epworth Press. Used by permission of The Macmillan Company, New York 11, N.Y.

PREFACE

Stars are divided by space, continents by water, nations by customs, people by class distinction. But time is divided by a Babe.

The miracle of that Babe's incarnation is a mystery. He differed from every other babe because He lived before He was born to Mary, and because He was spirit before He became flesh. Before He had existence here on earth, He had pre-existence. In his book *The Christ of the Gospels*, Dr. J. W. Shephard put this truth in a plain but polished way: "The how of [Christ's] incarnation is inscrutable; the why is incomprehensible; the fact is undeniable." Charles Wesley adds his quota thus:

> Our God contracted to a span,
> Incomprehensibly made man.

John the evangelist informs us that ten thousand things that Jesus Christ said and a thousand things that He did are not written in the Bible (John 20:30, 31; John 21:25). Never has a complete biography of Christ been written nor ever can one be written. Mortal pen can never fill in the hidden years in His life. What God has hidden let no man try to uncover by the faulty method of imagination.

Jesus Christ created no wars, He organized no armies, He advocated no force, He established no bands. He gathered no riches, He possessed no property, He demanded no tithes, He gave no bribes, He sought no favors, He coveted no honors. He wrote no books, organized no church, built no altars, performed no sacrifices, wrote no creed, formulated no ritual.

Jesus Christ was a King, but His manner of life contradicted all the accepted standards of kingship. He was a Ruler, but He held no courts. He fought the greatest enemy of mankind, but He never carried a sword. He could have had legions of angels to guard Him, but all His days He walked without human protection.

Part I of this book is a study of the three temptations of Jesus. Peter, in his first epistle, pictures the Son of God now become Son of man, draped in our flesh, combatting our temptations, and knowing the "contradiction of sinners against himself." Storms swept over His soul. More than once Jesus could say with the Psalmist, "All thy billows are gone over me." The deep experiences that befell Jesus are given to us unvarnished and without exaggeration. His sure anchorage was the unchangeable Word of God. He constantly stated, "It is written."

We think of Jesus Christ as our Lord and Saviour first, and then afterwards as our pattern Man, who came to show us how to live. "Christ . . . suffered for us," says Peter, "leaving us an example, that ye should follow in his steps." Then Peter lists several steps for us, His disciples, to follow:

> Who did no sin,
> neither was guile found in his mouth:
> who, when he was reviled, reviled not again;
> when he suffered, he threatened not;

but committed himself to him that judgeth righteously. —I Pet. 2:22, 23

Regarding temptation, we Christians might well say with Horatius Bonar: "It is the way the Master went. Should not the servant tread it still?" Since Jesus Christ not only conquered temptation but was more than conqueror, we too can have victory with a margin in every temptation. "As he is, so are we in this world."

The approach to the second study, the Transfiguration of Christ, was not planned. I feel somewhat like the man who one day when crossing a field (maybe when his spirits were down) stumbled over a pot of gold. Suddenly there seemed to be a challenge from the life of our incomparable Master to explore His transfiguration, a too-much-neglected crisis experience. I can only pray that from a close reading and meditation on this great theme, some of the rich perfume of God's grace that has entered my own soul will also be the lot of those who read these pages.

My feeling about this book is expressed in the words of Robert Southey:

> Go forth, little book, from this my solitude;
> I cast thee on the waters; go thy ways;
> And if, as I believe, thy vein be good,
> The world will find thee after many days.
> Be it with thee according to thy worth;
> Go, little book! In faith I send thee forth.

L. R.

Bethany Fellowship
Minneapolis, Minnesota
U.S.A.
April, 1963

CONTENTS

CHAPTER PAGE

THE TEMPTATIONS

Then Jesus was led by the Spirit up into the desert, to be tempted by the devil. After a fast of forty days and nights he was very hungry.

"If you really are the Son of God," said the tempter, coming to him, "tell these stones to turn into loaves."

Jesus answered, "The scripture says 'Man shall not live by bread alone, but by every word that proceedeth out of the mouth of God.' "

Then the devil took him to the holy city, and set him on the highest ledge of the Temple. "If you really are the Son of God," he said, "throw yourself down. For the scripture says— 'He shall give his angels charge concerning thee: and on their hands they shall bear thee up, lest haply thou dash thy foot against a stone.' "

"Yes," retorted Jesus, "and the scripture also says, 'Thou shalt not tempt the Lord thy God.' "

Once again the devil took him to a very high mountain, and from there showed him all the kingdoms of the world and their magnificence. "Everything there I will give you," he said to him, "if you will fall down and worship me."

"Away with you, Satan!" replied Jesus, "the scripture says, 'Thou shalt worship the Lord thy God, and him only shalt thou serve.' "

Then the devil let him alone, and angels came to him and took care of him.

—Matthew 4:1–11 *(Phillips)*

PART I — THE TEMPTATIONS

THE FIRST TEMPTATION

Then Jesus was led into the desert by the Spirit, to be tempted by the devil. He fasted forty days and forty nights and afterwards felt hungry. So the tempter came up and said to him, "If you are God's Son, tell these stones to become loaves." He answered, "It is written, 'Man is not to live on bread alone, but on every word that issues from the mouth of God.' "

—Matthew 4:1–4 (Moffatt)

Chapter 1

COMMAND THESE STONES

In Jesus' series of three temptations, the first one was to the strained, craving, natural appetite of hunger. "If thou be the Son of God," said the tempter, "command that these stones be made bread."

I have a private conviction that at the resurrection breakfast three years after the temptation, when Jesus called His disciples to eat, He did turn stones into bread. As the song says,

> There they met their hearts' desire,
> Bread and fish upon the fire.

Where did Jesus get that bread? I like to think that at that time He put a few stones in a row, and even as He had previously turned the water into wine exactly when it suited Him, so by turning stones into bread after His resurrection, He did a miracle both for His own convenience and to meet the needs of others. With a smile He said to the devil, "I do it when *I* want it done but not when *you* want it done." Be this conjecture of mine as it may, the fact is that in this wilderness experience, Jesus withstood the devil in the temptation to turn stones into bread.

At His birth the Saviour was not marred or scarred. Yet the Scriptures do say "his visage was so marred more than any man, and his form more than the sons of men." Did this facial disfigurement deduce partly from His forty days of wilderness fastings and wrestlings in prayer? We know the human body feels the wear and tear of a life spent in prayer and fasting. But under such spiritual discipline, one's soul expands. The Saviour was disfigured humanly but transfigured triumphantly.

The Bible says that originally the devil was the anointed cherub, with every precious stone for his covering. He was "full of wisdom and perfect in beauty"; he was "in Eden the garden of God" and "was perfect in [his] ways until iniquity was found in [him]." His downfall was pride, for the Word says, "Thine heart was lifted up because of thy beauty, . . . for thou hast said in thine heart, . . . I will exalt my throne above the stars of God: . . . I will be like the most High" (Ezek. 28:17; Isa. 14:13, 14).

Satan must have been a spectator of the glory which Christ had with the Father before the world was. When Jesus himself declared, "I beheld Satan as lightning fall from heaven," my opinion is that He was referring to His pre-human experience when Satan was cast out of heaven. When Christ was born, Satan must have seen and heard the heavenly host exulting, "Glory to God in the highest." He knew Christ had laid aside His glory for the task of world redemption. He must also have witnessed the baptism of Jesus and heard the voice which said, "This is my beloved Son." Therefore he must have known that Jesus was the living Son of the living God. The introductory phrase, "If thou be the Son of God," veils the devil's terror of God's Son. The devil's true concept is in his request: "Command that these stones be made bread."

There are two things about the devil I am sure of. First, though his agents may be operating simultaneously in a thousand places at once, the devil cannot be in two places at the same time or he would possess an attribute of God. (I am sure he does not possess that.) Second, the devil is smart enough to tempt us to do not what we can *not* do but what we *can* do. The latter was the devil's device in this first temptation. His subtle hope was that Jesus would not see that his was a hell-hatched scheme and that he purposed to induce Jesus to prove He was the Son of God and thus leave the realm of representative Man. But Jesus refused to step into the place of deity, even though it was in His power to do so. Through the last Adam, more was to be won back than what was lost through the first Adam. Indeed Isaac Watts put it in a superlative way:

In Him the tribes of Adam boast
More blessings than their father lost.

He "took on him the seed of Abraham," and this role He would not change to please a taunting devil.

Christ *was* the Son of God. I am sure the devil knew this at the time of Jesus' temptation. A little later, during Jesus' earthly life, he was to learn it more fully. At the end of this present age he will learn it eternally, for the Son of God did not yield to the bread-making scheme of the wilderness, and therefore the lake of fire will be the devil's eternal habitation. For a little season, Christ abode in the flesh. "Though he were a Son, yet learned he obedience by the things which he suffered; and being made perfect, he became the author of eternal salvation unto all them that obey him."

Jesus' triumph in this bread temptation, along with His triumph in other known and unknown temptations, gave Him the glorious classification of a High Priest who *can* be "touched with the feeling of our infirmities" and who was "in all points tempted like as we are, *yet without sin.*" One poet put it this way:

> "Who every grief hath known
> That wrings the human breast,
> And takes and bears it for His own
> That all in Him may rest."

"Emptied himself of all but love," says Charles Wesley. Voluntarily He stayed within the boundary of His self-appointed bondage to human personality. Benjamin Rhodes (1743) styled it "a servant's form He wore." He chose to stay in the class of a Son-servant. He rejected the devil's plea to exercise His equal-deity powers.

What was the real way out of this temptation to turn stone into bread? At least in human thinking, there seemed no other way but actually to turn stones into bread. The wilderness offered Jesus no fruit to eat. It was waste and howling and, as one writer puts it, "mysterious, utterly isolated, and infinitely remote." But Jesus did not have to eat at the devil's suggestion. In this uninhabitable, inhospitable, uncomfortable atmosphere, He had the greatest of human possessions—self-possession. He chose not to listen to the devil.

But why did He do so? He knew that if He lost in the wilderness, all men would have lost in Him; but if He won, then by faith all men could win in their wildernesses "according to the power that worketh in [them]." He knew that His obedience would bring to Him the kingdoms of this world "not for the years of time alone, but for eternity." It were better for Him to be hungry on earth for a little season and win this eternal reward rather than to succumb to bodily appetite, legitimate as that may have been, and lose the everlasting prize.

The first Adam failed because he disobeyed God and heeded the dull advice of the devil. Christ, the perfect Man, won because He rejected the terms of the devil and obeyed implicitly the will of His Father. Christ's abiding in the will of the Father meant His abounding in the Father for our account. His victory over this temptation meant that we too could have victory. In Romans 8:17 Paul gives this exalted phrase: "heirs; heirs of God, and joint-heirs with Christ."

After Jesus' forty days of battle, "he afterward hungered," says the record. It was real hunger to Jesus. These great biological drives were hurting. These legal appetites really called for satisfaction.

Do we know hunger? A short while ago I heard a good minister say what I am sure is true: "Most of us have never been hungry but have just had an appetite; we have never been thirsty but have just been dry." It is easy today for men who are full-bellied to legislate for thin men who are tormented daily by unsatisfied bodily hunger. In his remarkable little book, *He Sent Leanness*, David Head has this rather vicious humor listed as "A Prayer":

> We miserable owners of increasingly luxurious cars and ever-expanding television screens

> do most humbly pray for that two-thirds of the world's population which is under-nourished. *You can do all things, O God.* We who seek to maintain a shaky civilization do pray most earnestly that the countries which suffer exploitation may not be angry with the exploiters; that the hungry may not harbour resentment against those who have food; that the downtrodden may take it patiently; that nations with empty larders may prefer starvation to communism; that the "have-not" countries may rejoice in the prosperity of those that have; and that all people who have been deeply insulted and despised may have short memories. *You can do all things, O God.*

Mr. Head may have overdone this satire, but those of us who travel in these "backward countries" get his point clearly. The worldly-wise who watch travel films and TV newscasts know his meaning too. "Our daily bread" has become for all too many "our daily dread."

In the mercy of God this writer has seen many drunkards converted. Some of these have lost their craving for drink immediately—at the very first moment they rose from their altar of penitential prayer. Others have had to battle this appetite for months after their new experience of grace. It is easy for these lips of mine that have never tasted strong drink to tell a drunkard that he should have complete victory over drink with never a hangover longing lurking around. But for me to be so coldly philosophical about the issue does not help that struggling soul. When Satan treads on the holy ground of the soul's devotion, he does not take off the shoes from his feet, for he "cometh not, but for to steal, and to kill, and to destroy." In his diabolical strategy, whatever faith-destroying weapon is used, openly or secretly anything and all is fair.

We are all prone to cry out in the weakness of our flesh that there is a limit to human endurance in the time of trial—that is, a limit in the flesh. The body, we say, can take only so much beating and violence; then its resistance is exhausted. The mind, too, has a saturation point, so that after that the mind can take no more and sometimes operates on some very irrational levels.

I am thinking here that this very day as I write, some dear souls in inaccessible camps will be brainwashed by the Communists. Taunting men and scoffing demons will be the spectators of this modern technique of "education." By mere reasoning we do not understand this method nor know its meaning. Spiritually we know that "now we see through a glass darkly, but then face to face." The inspiring words of James Russell Lowell have new meaning these days:

By the light of burning martyrs,
  Christ, Thy bleeding feet we track,
Toiling up new Calvaries ever,
  With the Cross that turns not back.
New occasions teach new duties;
  Time makes ancient good uncouth;
They must upward still and onward
  Who would keep abreast of truth.

Though the cause of evil prosper,
  Yet 'tis truth alone is strong;
Though her portion be the scaffold
  And upon the throne be wrong—

Yet that scaffold sways the future,
And behind the dim unknown
Standeth God within the shadows,
Keeping watch above His own.

God judges now, but for those who abuse His children and His Church, He will pass judgment later.

Man's body does have limitations, but his spirit is capable of almost infinite endurance. By this we mean that where the Spirit is Lord of the personality, there does not need to be a breaking point in temptation. God is love. God indwelling the soul means that love beareth *all* things because God indwelling *can* bear all things.

Truth is many-sided. Might one thing which girded the Son of God in His onslaught with the devil have been the memory of other men's forfeitures? For little prizes they paid great prices! Did Jesus not hear again the cry of the bargaining Esau, who for a mess of pottage sold his birthright? Did the image of a shorn and sightless Samson pass before His vision? Would King Saul's bitter end fail to cross the intelligence of this tempted One? Could it be that in the silent acreage of the wilderness, Jesus heard King David's shattering wail of Psalm 51? Of these facts we are not sure, yet they are a distinct possibility.

Some take the attitude that with a mere shrug of the shoulder Jesus brushed off the devil's claim as beneath His serious consideration. But the whole weight of Scriptural evidence is against this shallow conception.

Who that is worth his salt has not been baffled by temptation? Who has not wondered at the "worthwhileness" of it? Who has not been teased by the apparent idleness of God, who could have swept away all the encountering forces of evil and opposition by the mere moving, as it were, of His little finger? (It is suggestive that Oswald Chambers calls his fine study of Job *Baffled to Fight Better*.)

Christ knew that His kingdom was not of this world. In times of temptation, was that thought always an anchor to His soul? Then should it not be an anchor to your soul and mine that as He is not of the world, so we are not of the world? We are in enemy territory. Like Bunyan's pilgrim, we are only passing through this Vanity Fair. We are to expect opposition and we are to expect acute temptation—unless we yield to the tempter and swear allegiance to his unholy cause. We need not be ignorant of the devil's devices. We do not have to fall into his snares, for if our wills are in line with the divine Will, we can resist and defeat the devil's will.

The three temptations faced by Jesus in the wilderness are not those faced by a child. Nor are they the temptations that challenge youth. They are full-grown temptations of full-grown men. Since in His humanity Christ's life was bounded by time, and since He too had normal propensities as a man, what repeated and unnamed conflicts He must have had! "Being found in fashion as a man," He faced all that we face. But in places where many of us have fallen, He fell not. Though His feet were very much on the earth, and His emotions must have risen and fallen as do ours. yet in all these things He triumphed gloriously.

After the Spirit manifested at the Jordan Jesus' anointing for the most amazing ministry the world has ever seen, does it bear thinking that Christ came behind in any of the gifts of I Corinthians 12? He certainly had the gift of wisdom in His gracious approach to the woman taken in adultery. He displayed supernatural knowledge when He directed a man to the place where a fish had the money for His income tax! He manifested power in that He raised the dead and healed the sick. His prophetic gift has lifted the veil for us on the end times, for He said, "So shall it be when the Son of man cometh." He displayed the gift of discerning of spirits, for He said of Nathanael, "Behold an Israelite indeed, in whom is no guile." Any or all of these gifts, manifested continually with increasing power, would get for Jesus world leadership. Is it unreasonable to think that in the wilderness He, the Son of God, was tempted to exploit these supernatural powers? Yet we know He turned from all exploitation in order to do the will of His Father.

The "drives" that surged through the natural bodies of other men must have been housed in the framework of the mortal body of the Son of God; otherwise this first temptation episode was burlesque. The devil knew better than to joke. He saw a fabulous prize if only the Christ could be tempted, tricked, and tripped. Then millions could be held captive.

However, Jesus battled against the devil with "the sword of the Spirit, which is the word of God." "*It is written!*" cried Jesus. The devil, therefore, had to leave the field of temptation. Is it a far-off guess that when this battering storm of temptation assailed Him alone in that wilderness, the reason He comforted His soul and denied himself bread was that He held to the rock of the truth in Psalm 2:8: "Ask of me, and I shall give thee the heathen for thine inheritance, and the uttermost parts of the earth for thy possession"? At any rate, we know that after Jesus wielded the Word of God, the devil was battered, though not shattered. He would try a second time.

Jesus returned from the Jordan full of the Holy Spirit and he was led by the Spirit to spend forty days in the desert, where he was tempted by the devil. He ate nothing during that time and afterward he felt very hungry.

"If you really are the Son of God," the devil said to him, "tell this stone to turn into a loaf."

Jesus answered, "The scripture says, 'Man shall not live by bread alone.' "

—Luke 4:1–4 (Phillips)

Chapter 2

NOT BY BREAD ALONE

Christ met the devil in the wilderness on the ground of His humanity, and replied to Satan's first temptation: "Man shall not live by bread alone." In an age mesmerized by materialism, we need to shout from the housetops the truth of Christ's reply: It is impossible to live by bread alone.

Note that Jesus did not say, "Man shall not live by bread." He added one word: "Man shall not live by bread *alone*." This is basically what modern man is trying to do—maintain life by material things. It is true that with all man's emphasis and maybe over-emphasis on life, he does not try to live by education alone. To ease pressure, the highbrow has the side vents of the country club, of sailing, or of golf. Then too, a man knows that he needs human love and so he takes unto himself a wife. Yet in common market language, modern man is a smart fool. All his life he wants to live, yet actually spends his time dying. Unless he accepts Christ as his Saviour, he lives without finding life.

This same modern man is the one who, with gracious condescension, has removed the Saviour title from Christ and replaced it with Teacher. Very well, we will for a moment accept that title of Teacher. One of Christ's teachings says, "Ye will not come to me that ye might have life." Another gem of His teaching is "I am . . . the life." He then clinched this claim with "I am the bread of life." It is true that man cannot live by bread alone. But it is equally true that without Christ, the true Bread sent down from heaven, man cannot live at all.

For thousands, the way to the psychiatrist's office is paved with aspirins; and for millions, the way to marital infidelity is paved with pulp magazines and third-rate films. For some, the way to hell is paved with formal religion; for others, with outright moral anarchy. But why, when the Bread of Life is there for the taking, does modern man insist on breaking his teeth chewing the stones of lifeless human philosophies?

Antoine de Saint Exupéry, in his *Letter to a General*, says, "Ah, there is only one problem, only one in all the world: How can we restore to man a spiritual significance, a spiritual discontent? Oh to let something descend upon them like the dew of a Gregorian chant. . . . Don't you see? We cannot live any longer on refrigerators, politics, balance-sheets, and crossword puzzles. We simply cannot."

There is a saturation point for human appetites. The sponge of our desires can take only so much. For some, after certain attainments, money ceases to have meaning and ambition's engine loses some of its drive. For others, the unreality of material conquest shows up in the language of the hymn by Henry F. Lyte: "Earth's joys grow dim, its glories pass away."

So we reiterate: Modern man needs this age-old counsel, "Man shall not live by bread alone." If he could gain the whole world, he would still be as unsatisfied as Alexander, crying because there were no more worlds to conquer. H. G. Wells was right in saying, "There is a God-shaped blank in us." That blank can be filled by God and by God alone. Man is so constituted that he has "an aching void which the world can never fill." Since man's need cannot be met by the bargain counters and the teamster's unions (plus country clubs and hunting trips), the church must leap into this challenging gap with a banquet of soul-food.

There are three challenging questions that all intelligent minds ask sooner or later. The child asks, "Where did I come from?" and a wise parent will prove his wisdom with a careful and intelligent answer. The parent can be sure that if he does not get this truth over to the child in the right way, somebody else will get it over in a wrong way.

The next question to the thinking soul comes in mid-life: "Why am I here?" This demands a better answer than the former question. John Wesley is said to have often quoted the saying of an old Quaker: "I shall pass this way but once; anything good therefore that I can do, let me do it, for I shall not pass this way again." This is good philosophy even if it does not carry a spiritual content.

The third question comes many many times in life. Sometimes it comes to the young (at least it came to me in very tender years) and grips the heart of the madcap youth. But more often it hangs over the mind like a cloud when the shadows lengthen. The question is this: "Where do I go from here?" In the breast of the believer this pertinent problem never raises a tremor. He knows whom he has believed. He knows he has passed from death to life. He also knows where he is going.

Man inhabits the flesh only for an interim period; he is made for eternity. But in man's effort to find life, he so often treads on pearls to reach for crab apples.

Of recent date there has been a whole crop of suicides by outstanding world personalities who, in the jargon of our day, "made it"—supposedly. But their untimely and self-inflicted deaths are a testimony to the truth that man cannot live either by bread or by success only. Their stark-naked emphasis is that with all their getting, they had garnered nothing of lasting worth. In their folly they have restated Solomon's words, "All is vanity." It is possible for a rotting fence to be brightened by another coat of paint, but it will fall just the same.

To cheer up a jaded spirit and an empty soul with the shallow laugh produced by a quip from a third-rate brain on TV only aggravates the craving that the God-empty heart knows. There are hungry souls amongst the crowd whose lingo has bingo and whose music is the tinkling of empty cocktail glasses. They are asking for bread. Yet from so many preachers they are getting only the juiceless stones of worldly wisdom. What a crying shame! Are empty pews a natural bonus for empty sermons? To us who minister the Word, I think the Master would say again and with some sternness, "Give ye them to eat." When we sing in church services William William's hymn,

> Bread of heaven, bread of heaven,
> Feed me now and evermore,

there is something more than a recitation of a hymn. There is a real hunger to be fed.

The husks that the world offers drive men to seek Bread. Would-be suicides may not know that their need is a personal Christ; neither do they have inward comfort at the thought of death and their leap in the dark. What they do know is that they do not have what it takes to meet the insatiable appetite that the leech of modern life would suck from them. This nervous generation, dragging its feet to the grave on supporting tranquilizers and antibiotics, is disturbed. A five-day week (with the promise of a four-day week in the not-far-distant future) has only thrown men into the dilemma of having more time to rest but nothing to rest on. They need Christ. They need the message of a vigorous church. They need to see a table prepared before them in the presence of their enemies. They need to "eat of his flesh and drink of his blood" that they might live. Ministers who fail to feed men with the Bread of Life feed men who will fail.

The pulpit must have pull, or else the pit will be filled. These are not just words for play but words that hurt and that challenge us to heart-searching and humble repentance. Men are not only spending money for that which is not bread but are spending non-returning time and their eternal souls for this life's vain mess of pottage. Collapsing human nature must somewhere find a Conqueror.

That answer is found in Jesus' wilderness temptation, for not only was the Spirit in Christ willing, but the flesh was strong. Christ's temptation occurred when the toil of His many hidden years was over. At the Jordan He must have been like some prince who, having traveled long in his father's kingdom, could not fail to be excited when the crown was finally put upon his brow. It was at Christ's baptism that His Father had placed upon His Son's brow the crown for ministry.

"The Spirit of the Lord God is upon me; because the Lord hath anointed me to preach good tidings unto the meek; he hath sent me to bind up the brokenhearted, to proclaim liberty to the captives, and the opening of the prison to them that are bound; to proclaim the acceptable year of the Lord, and the day of vengeance of our God; to comfort all that mourn" (Isa. 61:1, 2).

But in Jesus' hour of temptation, all this was fulfilled. If He failed here, the Scripture could not be fulfilled. An irate devil who had long been without a serious challenger to his power (there were 400 prophetless years between the Testaments) viewed with trembling concern the great stakes involved in his contest with One whom he knew to be the Son of God.

Would it be wrong to think that even in the preliminary round, Jesus was excited at the prospect of wresting the supremacy from the hands of the devil? I think not. Christ came into this world for this hour, the hour of His temptation, but also for redemption. At this juncture in His ministry, the Saviour must have known His redemptive mission. He must have known that "as in Adam all die, even so in Christ shall all be made alive." What a thrill to His soul to see that He could undo all that Adam had done!

"No man liveth unto himself"—not even Adam, not even Christ, nor this writer, nor you, my reader. Involved in my failure will be the failure of many others, and in my triumph the triumph of others. Christ therefore must have had an inner glow at the prospect of having won the first round in the forty days' temptation.

I run the race then with determination. I am no shadowboxer; I really fight! I am my body's sternest master, for fear that when I have preached to others I should myself be disqualified.

—I Corinthians 9:27 (Phillips)

No, I maul and master my body, lest, after preaching to other people, I am disqualified myself.

—I Corinthians 9:27 (Moffatt)

I bruise my body and make it my slave, lest possibly, after being a herald to others, I myself should be rejected.

—I Corinthians 9:27 (Weymouth)

Chapter 3

NOT MEAT AND DRINK

This chapter is a parenthesis. We digress from the main stream to a side stream of lesser importance, but of vital relationship to this book. It centers around a much-needed admonition: "The kingdom of God is not meat and drink."

The River Ganges is reputed to be sacred. We ourselves have seen its yellow waters—sacred to some, a drink for not a few, a bath for millions, and a bathroom for others. A chemist once analyzed some of the "sacred" waters, and the test showed the drop of water alive with bacteria. The shocked chemist called a Sadhu and had him peep through the microscope. He too saw the defiling germs. Then suddenly, while the chemist's back was turned, there was a crash. In anger the Sadhu had smashed the microscope. The view had been too revealing.

This is why sinners shun the Bible—it is too revealing. This is why believers back away from some Bible truths—they are too demanding.

Simplicity of living marked the earthly life of the Son of God This should mark our lives too. But does it? I am sure of this fact: If overeating were to get us Christians intoxicated, lots of us would be staggering around drunk! Yet from John the Baptist right down through the church ages, plain eating and plain living have marked the lives of many great Christian men. Moreover, the Son of God was conspicuous, but not by His "purple and fine linen." He was elegant in His homespun gown.

Whenever the Bible holds out rewarding promises either for this life or for the next, it is a delightful book to us. But when it touches on the body or on that manner of life that would mark us as daring to differ from the status quo in Christian circles, we say that the Bible needs "interpretation."

"The kingdom of God is *not* meat and drink," says the Apostle Paul. Entrance into God's kingdom, therefore, is not by closely following an exacting law at a meal table. On the other hand, the lavish, overloaded table that many of us keep is not in itself a sign of how good the Lord is to us. If such a table were the sign of God's blessing, what is it that displeaseth the Lord so that millions who love Him are half fed, half starved, and half dead? The kingdom of God is manifestly not meat and drink.

Neither is the kingdom entered by fasting. Yet I personally believe that all who want to live the Bible standard of Christianity will fast. Jesus, who said, "When ye pray. . . ," also said, "*When ye fast. . . .*" He did not say *if* ye pray or fast, but *when* ye pray and fast. Jesus seemed to take it for granted that, following in His steps and in His pattern of life, His children would pray and fast. Fasting gives time to get quiet.

Fasting gives opportunity for prayer. Let us each examine ourselves sometime and with a watch in our hands, take time to note how much time we spend in eating, and maybe how little or no time is spent for fasting.

First of all, the word fasting suggests being disengaged from the routine of life and having time for meditation and contemplation. Secondly, fasting suggests that a person has dominion over the strong appetite of eating. Fasting also denotes some permissible anxiety of spirit, some task to be done, some burden being carried, some shame in the spiritual realm that needs to be removed. Furthermore, fasting in the New Testament sense means obedience, for one can hardly go wrong in following the steps of the Master! Let me speak from experience and say that *all* the great saints I have known have been fasting people. Mr. Wesley used to say, "*All* good Methodists give at least two days a week to fasting."

The flesh does not choose fasting of itself. Many look upon it as monastic or legal. Not so. Strangely enough, in Paul's listing of the many things he suffered for the gospel's sake, he includes fasting: "In weariness, . . . in watching often, in hunger and thirst, *in fastings often*" (II Cor. 11:27). This was no isolated experience but seems to have been in the pattern of Paul's spiritual life.

In a certain missionary training school in England, staff and students fast each Friday. For thirty years this has been the pattern there. From that school men and women have gone to the ends of the earth. A world-famed missionary statesman and author of many books said that his society has had its best students and missionaries from that school. Blessed are they who learn this secret weapon of fasting even while they are in training, and then keep it up right through life!

Mastering the appetite for food helps master other appetites too. Self-possession is the best possession that man has. Fasting fortifies man in the realm of self-control. Though one part of self-control is fasting from food, there is also fasting from the company of others, even as our Lord in the wilderness had with Him no Peter or James or John.

I had the pleasure of pastoring a church where one day a week was given to prayer and fasting. We met in the church any time after nine o'clock in the morning. Anyone could come and fast and pray for the whole day or for any part of it. The cost of the missed meal was estimated and that money was dropped into a box designated for foreign missions. I have never forgotten the blessedness and power in that church. God wrought great things. I recommend this method to others.

In this writer's mind, there is no doubt at all that the "breakfast" and "banquet" idea in the church has outlasted its usefulness and in many cases has become a positive menace. Paul warned the hungry to eat at home. If the only fire a church has is in its kitchen and not upon its altar, then God pity that church. Any experience I have had at such an event (with a few exceptions) has left me with little appetite to be invited again. Most of the time is taken up with eating, with "star" singers, with a joking chairman, with an appeal (usually too long) for financial support, and then with a get-it-over-quickly attitude to the message. Sometimes there was also this side-whisper to the speaker: "It would be good not to be too outspoken just now because there are non-churchgoers here, and besides, those of other faiths might be offended." The fact is that compromise has changed its coat and talks today about toleration in honeyed terms.

There is also fasting from speaking. In the middle of the Welsh revival, press agents sought out its leader, Evan Roberts, for some information. But Roberts would not speak. Instead, he wrote on a paper that the Lord had told him to keep a fast of silence for seven days. Having ears, Evan Roberts had heard what the Spirit had said and he had obeyed.

One of the trite sayings among believers is this: "the world, the flesh, and the devil." The flesh and the devil have come in for many definitions and expositions. But it is the word *world* that gets far beyond our lines of interpretation. Let us consider it in some detail.

What tinseled explanations one hears of the text "Love not the world." Some preachers have blasted at wedding rings as the church's chief cause of offence to God. At the same time, many of those who hold strongly against a little strip of gold on one finger, grasp madly with both hands at gold in any other form. They live ostentatiously and extravagantly.

Does any person, I wonder, keep the exact letter of the Word of God? For instance, who does not have two coats? Well, I know a few who keep the letter of the Word, but they are very few. Almost all of them are outside England and America. Right away I know the replies that some would throw at me. They would say this: "What kind of world would it be if people did not buy this or if they did not do that?" My answer would be that we are not talking about the world but about the church. Alas, in the realm of materialism there is almost no line of demarcation between the living of a believer and a worldling.

It is my deep conviction that today the Bible is suffering not only from the liberal's interpretation but also from rationalization by the folk in the deeper-life bracket. Take the case of the interpretation of Pentecost. A brother fiercely assailed me because a friend of mine in preaching on Acts 2:4 ("They were all filled with the Holy Ghost and began to speak with other tongues") dealt with the first half of the verse but ignored the second. "This is bad exposition," said the complaining brother. He was right, I am sure. But (and this consideration is essential) if the one preacher is dishonest who treats only one half of a text, is another not dishonest also who ignores or purposely avoids the context of the whole chapter? Acts 2:4 is true but so is 2:44: "All that believed were together, and had all things common." Some old saint said that unless a man's pocket is converted, he is not very far converted. For many of us today, obedience to Acts 2:44 would be a severe test.

I am writing this chapter during Christmas week. My dim eyes do not fail to see that even among believers there is a spirit of covetousness abroad. Few are "hoping for nothing." To many Christians, the joy of giving is surpassed by the hope of getting. I do not hold a brief for the nuns or for the Amish people. Though they are miles apart in doctrine, I do admire one point about them both—they have dared to hold to an old, conventional, modest form of dress. (The Salvation Army might also come in for this same commendation.) What a touchy subject dress is! But those who are not condemned will not complain.

I was raised in a church where each time we met at the Lord's table, the whole chapter eleven of First Corinthians was read soberly and without comment. From that day to this, whenever we meet at the communion table, I have never been reconciled to the popular reading of only the last half of this chapter. Scriptures that hurt, we weakly avoid.

It seems to me that the burden of New Testament writers was to remind believers and then reiterate to them that their safety was not in getting as near the world as possible, but in being *in* the world yet not *of* it.

There is no question that this flabby age (I mean this age of flabby Christians) does not take to suffering at all. It is not easy, therefore, to counter the world's argument that most Christians are trying to make the best of both worlds. Amidst the rubble of shattered Germany, Dr. Helmut Thielicke, the famed Lutheran minister of Hamburg, Germany, "kept his head" and his feet. Before his nation prostrated, he stood up against Hitler with great moral power and spiritual strength, and so he knows whereof he speaks. Heed then this word from Dr. Thielicke's book, *The Waiting Father*, about nations who call themselves Christian: "I am afraid the Communists will hold their noses at the vile-smelling wealth of the man who has squandered his father's capital and then goes blabbing around a battlefield *with a few decayed Christian ideas.* Europe, the 'Christian' West, threatens to become something impossible to believe" (page 23).

This is true not only of Europe, for that last sentence might be tagged on to "Christian" England and "Christian" America too. Their honeymoon, also, is over. Thielicke's phrase "a few decayed Christian ideas" slays me. Is that his subtle way of saying we Christians have theories—splendid and wonderful theories of Christianity—in our minds that are mere eggs that have never hatched out into practical living?

Africa is stretching herself out, and in the future, by one method or another, will surely get what she could have already had by proper Christian administration. (This is true of other nations too.) Many people sneered when "the welfare state" began in England, but a prominent socialist hit back at these scoffers by saying something to this effect: "If you Christians had loved one another and had not continued to see your brother in need, there would have been no need for socialism. And," he added, "since you will not do it by love, we socialists will take from 'the haves' by force and give to 'the have nots.' "

After one of his world trips, Dr. Billy Graham told an American audience that all people in this country are millionaires; and in the general sense, he was right. This meat-and-drink side of life has become not a blessing but a bane to many. The kingdom of God is *not* meat and drink.

We believe that fasting is part of the harness that the Lord would have us wear. Fasting helps keep the body under. Yet, remember, the Pharisees did a share of fasting too. That did not shield them from the blast of Christ's condemnation: "ye are like unto whited sepulchres."

Fasting might be called a tithing of the appetite. But though they paid that tithe (and other tithes too), the Pharisees were despised by God and by man. Because these men used tithes falsely, we are not to despise them altogether. "What therefore God hath joined together, let not man put asunder."

The faultless humanity of our blessed Lord is a constant challenge and rebuke to us. Christ had an utter contempt for the gilded materialism which in His day soiled the temple courts with its merchandise and broke the sanctity of the Lord's courts with the jingle of the trading shekels.

Christ was accused of being a winebibber, and yet He was untroubled at the accusation. He consorted with publicans and with sinners; He also withdrew from them and from the disciples for lonely prayer on the mountainside. Such was His mastery of His bodily appetites and emotions.

God the Holy Spirit cannot be tied down to a place. "Neither in this mountain, nor yet at Jerusalem" is the place where men can worship. The hollow-eyed anchorites did not by their mere abstentions glorify the Lord. Monasticism became fat and corrupt. Conformity to a man-made standard in dress or do's and don't's cannot produce spirituality. By merely conforming to any or all of these standards, we cannot claim spirituality. "God is a Spirit: and they that worship him must worship him in spirit and in truth." Our supreme need is Christ.

"Less than Thyself, O do not give;
In might Thyself within me live.
Come, all Thou hast and art."

THE SECOND TEMPTATION

Then the devil took him to Jerusalem and set him on the highest ledge of the Temple. "If you really are the Son of God," he said, "throw yourself down from here, for the scripture says, 'He shall give his angels charge concerning thee, to guard thee,' and 'On their hands they shall bear thee up, lest haply thou dash thy foot against a stone.'"

To which Jesus replied, "It is also said, 'Thou shalt not tempt the Lord thy God.'"

—Luke 4:9–12 (Phillips)

Chapter 4

MIRACLE FOR MIRACLE'S SAKE?

The devil's plan is to wreck men—any men, all men. His greatest prize would have been the collapse of the moral and spiritual power of the Man among men, even the Son of God. In the first temptation we saw that the devil attacked the Saviour on the physical level. The emphasis seemed to be on Christ's power and position: "If *thou* art the Son of God." It was not Christ's position alone that the devil was considering but also His possible perversion of it. In the second temptation the devil switched his method. He set Christ on a pinnacle of the temple and said to Him, "If thou be the Son *of God*, cast thyself down." Here the devil changed the emphasis. The temptation now was not that the Son use His own power but that He test His Father's power.

It is remarkable to note in the Scriptures that the voice of the devil is heard on only three occasions. First, in the Garden of Eden he tempted man to disbelieve and disobey God, for he said to Eve, "Hath God said?" Here the devil accused God before man. Next, concerning the life of Job, a servant of God, Satan answered the Lord and said, "Doth Job serve God for nought?" Here the devil accused man before God. Thirdly, at the temptation of Jesus Christ, the devil again spoke, and this time directly to the tempted One. He wanted the Son of God to step outside His rightful privilege and cast himself down from the pinnacle in order to accuse the God-man of disobedience.

The devil took Jesus into Jerusalem, the holy city, and set Him upon a pinnacle of the temple. God's people, Israel, loved this city. David the Psalmist forthrightly declared, "If I forget thee, O Jerusalem, let my right hand forget her cunning. If I do not remember thee, let my tongue cleave to the roof of my mouth" (Ps. 137:5). Jesus himself in His early years must have often heard a temple choir sing concerning Jerusalem: "Beautiful for situation, the joy of the whole earth, is mount Zion"; and again, "They that trust in the Lord shall be as mount Zion which cannot be removed." To the Jew, Palestine was dear, for by inheritance this land was his. The center of the beloved country was Jerusalem; the center of Jerusalem was the temple. Jesus loved the temple.

Whether or not Herod's temple from which Jesus was told to cast himself down had pinnacles is not the point. One marginal reading offers the word "wing" instead of pinnacle. The temple's southern wing beside Herod's royal portico had been made magnificent. Josephus says, "Anyone standing on the extreme eastern end of the portico and looking down would be giddy. . . ; his sight could not reach to such an immense depth." Dr. J. W. Shephard says, "This wing was the watch-post, where the white-robed priests customarily called the people to the early worship and the priests to the morning sacrifice, as the massive temple gates swung open ere sunrise."

The devil, who had tried in the first temptation to get Jesus to distrust the plan of God, tried in the second one to get Jesus to dare God: "Cast thyself down: for it is written, He shall give his angels charge concerning thee." This promise in Psalm 91:11, 12, from which the devil was quoting, is a promise of providential care in an emergency, not a promise of deliverance in a situation of deliberate recklessness. James, the brother of Jesus, thrown down from this pinnacle or wing some thirty-eight years after Jesus' temptation, was dashed onto the rocks 450 feet below and killed.

In this age when the church is getting soaked with sensationalism of a low and unspiritual caliber, we need to rethink a few things. Why did Jesus take a lowly route of the incarnation? Why choose the slow and maybe poverty-lined years of the carpenter's cottage? Why not receive fame as a king at once? Examine this second temptation. Suppose Jesus had wanted to win the people by a magic operation, defying the laws of gravity and human suffering by throwing himself down from above. Instead of this display to a few hundred people, why not give a full-scale demonstration that millions might see? Why not split the skies in the fiery chariot in which Elijah went up into heaven and descend some black night, preceded by the voice of an archangel? What a sight it would have been if the Son of God had flung himself from the temple height and landed unscathed amidst the people. Crowds all over Palestine would immediately see Him descend.

Right away they would identify the chariot as a heavenly transport, would worship Him, and in this startling manifestation of power would make Him king. Why not be sensational? Because this was not the will of the Father. To the Son of God, that was the crux of the whole matter. Miracle for miracle's sake was not of interest to Jesus. A miracle alone is not the way to win the people.

Jesus knew His own miracle power. On one occasion He walked on water, yet most times He took a boat. But why take a boat when He had the miracle power to walk on water? Because only when He himself wanted to, would He do miracles and revert every law of nature, not when the devil said, "Cast thyself down," or when men taunted, "Come down from the cross."

Christ's life was a pageant of miracles. He was born in a miracle—He was conceived by the Holy Ghost. His death was a miracle—it atoned for the sins of men. His resurrection was a miracle—the law of death was broken and reversed. His ascension was a miracle—He contradicted the law of gravity. His second coming will be a miracle too—He will defy the law of gravity again. Miracles Christ did; miracles Christ will do—but not for the sake of charming the crowd and gaining adherents. Only as Christ dwelt in the secret place of the most High could He abide under the protecting shadow of the Almighty. The strong tower into which the righteous hide and are safe is the core of God's will. This safety in the will of God was true for the Son of God. It is also true for the sons of God.

The name used for Satan in Christ's temptations in the wilderness is devil, meaning "slanderer" or "false accuser." It may not be unreasonable to suggest that the devil has not gone out of business as the "accuser of the brethren," and may still have access to God to accuse us before Him. If at the judgment seat of Christ the devil will be called to be a witness, even there he may still try to accuse us. Certainly he now gets plenty of help from the saints who, not smart enough to detect his wiles, impute wrong motives to others and also misjudge even their own motives, and often fall for Satan's guile.

Some people say the devil has been after them all day. What conceit! Are they so mightily dangerous that Lucifer has to trail them for hours? Would to God they were! If the devil followed them all day, he would have to leave others alone. Their torment of spirit could be due to the work of a lesser evil spirit, the oppression from wicked people, their own dark impressions, or their toying with the occult. Can the devil be in two places at once? If so, I say again that he must possess an attribute of God. This is not so, for Satan is limited to a one-place abode. Likewise he does not have the knowledge that many of us attribute to him, for I do not believe that he knows the future except in a very limited sense.

The devil's second request of the Son of God was "Cast thyself down from here." In this temptation the devil infers that if Christ will obey and show off His great miracle power before the crowd ready to throng the temple, then they will believe that He is the One anointed to deliver the nation and restore the long-dreamed-of kingdom. But miracles did not convince His disciples. Even after three years of close ministry with the Son of God just prior to Pentecost, His disciples were still asking, "Wilt thou at this time restore the kingdom to Israel?"

Even with its long history, ritual, and veneration, the temple in Jerusalem was not hallowed to the devil. Would it be wrong to say that from the pulpits inside today's temples the devil can often get his plans supported? Because many servants of the Lord have listened to the devil's voice and fallen for his bait, have they not thrown themselves down from heights of hard-won popularity into the devil's scrap heap? A world-famed preacher from London told me that some of his most awful thoughts came to him as he ministered the sacrament in his large church. There is no ground hallowed to the devil. There is no place that the devil will not invade. There is no person that the devil will not follow to the very grave in order to get him to doubt God or rebel against His plan.

Few things sting a strong man more than the suggestion that he is a coward. Was this the Evil One's accusation to Jesus? Did he infer or even say that Jesus was afraid to cast himself down and so cast himself on God?

We cannot overemphasize the method that Jesus used to destroy this work of the devil. To the first temptation Jesus said, "It is written." In the second He said, "It is written again" (Matt. 4:7). What a shield of faith the Word of God is against all the fiery darts of the Evil One! God's Word is settled in heaven. God has no need to change His Word. God has no improvements to make in it, no revisions to give it, no more additions to make to it. His Word is complete, final, infallible. His Word is what Mr. Gladstone, a prime minister of England, called "the impregnable rock of

Holy Scripture." We believe the Word of God in order to be wise; we practice it in order to be holy.

THE THIRD TEMPTATION

Then the devil took him up and showed him all the kingdoms of mankind in a sudden vision, and said to him: "I will give you all this power and magnificence, for it belongs to me and I can give it to anyone I please. It shall all be yours if you will fall down and worship me."

To this Jesus replied, "It is written, 'Thou shalt worship the Lord thy God and him only shalt thou serve.' "

—Luke 4:5–8 (Phillips)

Chapter 5

THE LURE OF POWER

Time was running out for the archenemy of Christ. Two attempts to divert the Son from the will of the Father have blown back in Satan's face. He is smarting now—balked, but not yet admitting defeat. He will make one last great throw, this time in another realm of temptation. Because Christ had taken upon himself the form of a servant, the devil will now offer Him power as a king.

We do not know how this temptation was put over to the Saviour, and whether or not from the heights of Quarantania the devil actually showed Jesus the unveiling of the kingdoms of this world. Some have suggested that from these mountain heights where the temptation took place, Jesus could see many converging caravan routes bringing in their treasures and costly spices from the East, and that by these Satan would impress Christ with the great power and possessions of nations afar off. But this is hardly a satisfying interpretation.

Another way for the devil to show the kingdoms to Jesus would be by word pictures. There are times when, through the medium of words and without a sketch or artist's drawing, we "show" someone a project or a plan along with its detailed explanation. Was some such glorious picture what Satan used? A third way could have been by means of an apocalypse or revelation.

It seems to me that the final kingdom offer in this series of three temptations is the highest point, the apogee. There was nothing provincial here. Though temporal in nature, this offer was vast.

With the first Adam, Satan "worked his trick." The offer was that if Adam and Eve would eat of the tree of the knowledge of good and evil, they then would be "as gods." In other words, power, great power, would then be theirs. The last Adam would not fall for a like offer of power.

The devil "shewed unto Jesus all the kingdoms of the world in a moment of time." In that day, the might of Rome was stretching far away from Jerusalem. Perhaps Jesus was shown the splendor of Rome as its soldiers marched through the streets of the holy city, Jerusalem, with the Roman eagle flying over it and Roman rulers ordering its way of life. The devil's third offer was this: "All this power [of Rome, of Greece, etc.] will I give thee, and the glory of them: for that is delivered unto me; and to whomsoever I will I give it. If thou therefore wilt worship me, all shall be thine." In other words, if Christ would only yield to Satan, then Satan would let Him have power over the rulers of Rome. Wasn't power what the Jews wanted—power to be delivered from oppressors? Such a deliverer they would also worship.

The glory of Greece, though now almost completely passed away, was also in Satan's package deal. Moreover, in the immediate land of Palestine and within Christ's reach were the discordant elements of the Herodians, Essenes, zealots, scribes, Sadducees, and Pharisees. These also could serve Jesus and kneel to His power. Jesus could smash emperor worship in the Roman Empire. He could liberate the slaves, of which there were more than six million in this empire alone. These would then worship Him. All these kingdoms, plus all the wealth of the nations, Satan offered to Jesus in order to get what he had always wanted—worship. On two points the devil had failed to seduce the Master. Now he threw off his guise and made this third terrible offer: "If thou wilt worship *me*, . . ." The issue was out in the open. Again a fallen son of God and God's only begotten Son would lock in holy war.

Years before, Satan had fallen from his first estate because he desired to be as God. He had coveted the worship that angels, seraphim, and mortals gave to the Father and to the Son, the glory which Jesus had with Him "before the world was." Later when Satan seduced the first Adam, he gained great control. If he could now get the allegiance of the last Adam, he would get greater power. If Jesus Christ would bow the knee to the devil, all the kingdoms would be His.

In this battle for supremacy, the Prince of Peace and "the prince of the power of the air" were having a final round. One or the other must retire discredited. Neither wanted to do so. This was not a battle of mere strength, not a display of spiritual jujitsu. Kingdoms were involved here. Millions of souls born and unborn were to read the final outcome. Millions were to share in the ultimate triumph and defeat. Satan was willing to gamble away his temporal rights if only he could keep his grip on the millions for whom he bids and take them to habitations of eternal darkness.

But Jesus was not to be led astray. He saw beyond the devil's present offer to the time when every knee, including the devil's, would bow to Him. A couple of years later Jesus said concerning the devil, "The prince of this world cometh, and hath nothing in me." What utter futility there was in the devil's third temptation! It was not impossible for Christ to sin. But it was possible for Him not to sin. This possibility He gloriously displayed.

Not only those kingdoms that could be seen but those of generations unborn were in this offer. The first Adam's temptation looks tawdry in the light of the last Adam's temptation. Yet the first man failed; the last Man won. He commanded the devil to depart: "Get thee hence." To do the same is within the circumference of the possibilities and privileges of all Christ's disciples.

The question again might be asked: "Do we push the devil around, or does he push us around?" Maybe in this wilderness conflict the enemy thought he was wearing down the Son of God. The fact was that Christ was exposing the fallacy of the devil in thinking he could divert a soul who was set to do the Father's will. The exceeding great and precious promises given to the Son of God include the joy of being "the head and not the tail" in the matter of temptation.

How can this third temptation be applicable to our lives? To us believers there are offers galore if only we will substitute what we have in the Spirit for something in the shape of power that the world has to offer. I remember well a man whose feet were plucked from the miry clay and set upon the rock. For a time he walked very well; then he was introduced to a secret society where he found fellowship of a kind—a kind that strengthened his business connections. He got more on his feet but less on his knees. Then came the night when the Holy Spirit faced him with the choice of making a break with this secret society. By the eye of memory I can see that man now. He was tense. His face was white. The battle was fierce. I feel he lost it, for since that day he has never counted much for God.

Our temptations vary. One man's specific temptation may be to follow a career and thereby give God more money to send others to the mission field. God's answer to this temptation is in Samuel's words: "To obey is better than sacrifice, and to hearken than the fat of rams."

If we wholly follow the Lord, there is nothing in our lives that the death-dealing cross will not need to enter. Either the Spirit, or self, or the devil holds the overlordship of man's tripartite being. If there is any dual leadership, there can be no abiding blessing and no real progress in growth in grace. To follow the Lord means every vestige of self must go. Self must not have dominion, and Satan must not have dominion! To follow Christ means He alone must reign and rule. Blessed is the man who can say through the blood of Christ, "The prince of this world cometh, and hath nothing in me."

There is no exemption from temptation. It is something we Christians have to live with. At times the devil may switch from temptation to what Peter calls "the trial of your faith"—bodily affliction, or loss in business life, or slander, or false accusation. Even in these trials we are but following the Master's steps.

I think the devil pulls no greater trick with the Christian than in the realm of feelings. Sometimes a Christian does not "feel" the Lord is present or does not "feel" saved. But does a man have to feel married in order to be married? On this winter day in which I am writing, am I right in concluding that because the clouds are completely hiding the sun, there is no sun? No. The clouds will yet move; the sun will yet shine. Often the Lord's face seems to be hidden, so that when Satan comes saying, "You deserve better treatment from the Lord's hand," we are tempted to doubt.

In I Peter 1:6 we are told that for a season we may be in heaviness "through manifold temptations." Different translations of this verse in the New Testament put no new slant on it. The dictionary helps more because it says manifold means many varieties of temptations. Temptations to bodily appetites, temptations to the Spirit, or temptations to the mind—all these can bring heaviness.

Heaviness, then, is consistent with a Spirit-filled life. The plagues on Christ's spirit during this wilderness temptation may well have caused Him much heaviness of spirit. On a later occasion, Scripture says He began to be sorrowful and very heavy. Was He less filled with the Spirit then, than on other occasions?

Feelings are the least and the last thing in which a believer can put his trust. Some temptations are due to bodily pressures; others come with the arrival of bad news and the like. But if one has retained his integrity and is walking in all the known will of the Lord, he can snub his own feelings. He can say, "It is written!" and find the Word of God to be the sheet anchor of his soul.

The limits to satanic craftiness are unknown to us. But this we do know: Satan has many wiles. Over against all these, the Book says we need not be ignorant of Satan's devices. One way to keep informed on satanic strategy is to keep close to the Word of the Lord, for throughout the ages we find in the Word the exposure of devil craft. He has little if anything new to try. Does he assail thy soul? Then adopt the Psalmist's method—"I will say to my soul." Tell yourself that you are treading a path well-worn down the ages by the feet of the saints. Before you were ever born, some struggling saint had this very temptation of yours tried on him. He "made it" in the Spirit. So can you. Be sure of this: God is not capricious. There is no guesswork with Him. To Him you are more precious than ten thousand worlds, for you were purchased by the blood of His dear and only begotten Son.

> ". . . behind the dim unknown,
> Standeth God among the shadows
> Keeping watch upon His own."

On earth "we see through a glass darkly"—sometimes very darkly. Through the gloaming there seems to be no image, no reason for the prolonged soul torture, no easy explanation, indeed no explanation at all for the extended provocation to the soul. But "He silently worketh for thee." Forty days of temptation for the Son of God was a long time. Out of a three-year ministry it looked like an unnecessary probation, or at least too long a one. This thought brings the word of the poet to mind:

> "Judge not the Lord by feeble sense
> But trust Him for His grace;
> Behind a frowning providence
> He hides a smiling face."

In the Epistle of James there are many pearls of truth. Chapter one, verse two, says, "My brethren, count it all joy when ye fall into divers temptations." Again in verse twelve, James shows that "the man that endureth temptation . . . *shall receive the crown of life*, which the Lord hath promised to them that love him." There are compensations for protracted testings. Conversely, those who love Him get extended temptations!

As children in England we used to sing a rollicking song of former days: "Hearts of oak are our ships." Of their mighty oak trees, the English are proud. I am told that the young oak when planted will drive deep down into the earth and where possible get its roots linked like locked fingers around some great rock. The rock is its anchor. The tree on the edge of the forest gets the brunt of the storm and the lashing of the gale. It bucks and tosses in the gusts of wind; it creaks and groans under the temper of the storm. But it gets a real compensation—it is the tree that has the best graining in its wood. As it twists and heaves to the shock of the threatening wind, its very life is enriched.

Why do we reach on the shelf for this particular book or for that one? Usually because it is the record of a storm-tossed soul. Here is the story of a missionary movement shipwrecked on God, and there an account where we tread the lonely road of a soul who in his lifetime hungered, or else was slandered and ridiculed or gossiped about by stay-at-home, armchair, weak-kneed Christians. As the story of Palissy says,

> When he was living, he hungered for bread;
> They gave him a statue when he was dead.

Thus it has been with many a saint. Time has given perspective to his faith, his courage, his self-abnegation. Blessed be the Lord for all He has wrought through frail flesh—cleansed, sanctified, and meet for the Master's use!

If the matter were left with us, we might choose to be without temptation. The devil offered Christ a world with a crown on it and victory (so the offer said) without a Gethsemane or a Calvary. For a far less bargain many a man has fallen for earthly power and favor.

But Jesus overcame the devil every time, in every place, and on every level. My heart rises in praise to Him for this. Christians bow their knees to God the Father because His Son did not bow the knee to the tempting devil. We sing in triumph with John Ellerton:

> So be it, Lord; Thy throne shall never,
> Like earth's proud empires, pass away;
> Thy kingdom stands and grows forever,
> Till all Thy creatures own Thy sway.

Pilate was right to slip a bit of paper over the cross on which Christ's crime was identified: "This is Jesus the King of the Jews." But Pilate's words fell far short. It should have read, as does "Te Deum":

> Thou art the King of glory, O Christ;
> Thou art the everlasting Son of the Father.
> When Thou tookest upon Thee to deliver man,

Thou didst not abhor the virgin's womb.
When Thou hadst overcome the sharpness of
death,
Thou didst open the kingdom of heaven to all
believers.

There is a record somewhere of Luther's saying that Isaiah 53 is so precious that it should be written on gold for parchment and lettered with diamonds. This statement is true also of much of the Word of God. A shining example of the priceless value of the Word of God is James 4:7: "Submit yourselves therefore to God. Resist the devil, and he will flee from you." Could anything be clearer than this promise of victory in the hour of temptation? Because we have not used the weapon of this mighty promise of God in our conflict with our archenemy, have we suffered setback and downright defeat? Christ's shield of faith is "It is written," and "It is written again."

What a woeful task a man has if he enters a conflict with the miserable inward conviction that he is going to lose! If he enters the battle with a sense of having an equal chance to win, he is better disposed to fight. If he enters the fray with a knowledge that he has superior power and therefore *will* win, the encounter is a delight. He has inward joy that he *can* subdue his enemy. I believe Jesus, coming as He did to the temptations from the place of the Spirit's anointing, knew that He could overcome all the wiles of the devil.

In this wilderness contest with the enemy, Jesus relied on one thing and one thing only—the immutable Word of God. He did not mention His feelings at all, though during that forty days' spell His feelings must have been great and diverse. He had no friend to counsel with. His sole foundation of faith and weapon for victory was "It is written." As our method of defense, we have this same Word, this unchanged promise. As our weapon of attack, we have this same power of the Spirit.

It is as he suffered by his temptations that he is able to help the tempted.

—Hebrews 2:18 (Moffatt)

He himself has shared full in all our experience of temptation, except that he never sinned.

—Hebrews 4:15b (Phillips)

Chapter 6

TEMPTED IN ALL POINTS

We need to be reminded that Jesus was led into the wilderness not by the devil, as is so often quoted, but by the Spirit. Nor did He return into Galilee a near wreck from exhaustion. As Luke gives in a valuable postscript, He returned "in the power of the Spirit" (Luke 4:14). He returned "more than conqueror." *He* was the victor and the devil the vanquished.

Jesus was in the wilderness forty days, tempted of Satan. In this tract of time, how many temptations were there? Just three? Or were there thirty-three? Or three hundred and three? (This is not a rhetorical question.) Apparently it was *after* the forty days' temptation that the devil pestered Jesus to turn stones into bread, then goaded Him to throw himself from the pinnacle of the temple in a miracle display, and finally offered Him the kingdoms of this world.

If these three temptations came *after* the forty days of temptation (and the inspired Word says that they did—Luke 4:2), then what happened during the forty days? What was the range of temptation that the Holy One outlasted and trampled under foot? Over that whole period, the Scriptures are silent; at least there is no explanation of them in the context of the temptation record. Hebrews 4:15 says, "He was *in all points* tempted like as we are, yet without sin." This must mean that the Son of God was tempted through the over-all experiences of life that befell Him. During nights spent in prayer there may have been many unlisted temptations. Some of the enemy's fiercest attacks come when we seek to get away from him and be alone with God, for the devil has an unblushing arrogance and a penetrating oppression. To him, the prayer closet is not sacred—witness his desecration of the hallowed spot of Gethsemane. Some believers hope to get out of the complete reach of temptation in this life, but they cherish an idle hope. The Son of man was tempted; the sons of men will be tempted. He was victor in all His temptations; we too can know perfect victory.

Since the devil could not triumph over the Saviour by direct attacks, he next tried an indirect line. We read that some time afterwards, men sought to make Jesus king without the cross. A little later on, in the blazing glory of Christ's transfiguration, there was no near presence of the devil at all, though there could have been inner pressure on Him to step back with Moses and Elijah into heaven.

The devil's final assault on the Son of God came in Gethsemane. Somebody has said that the British do not win battles, but they do win wars. In other words, they may lose the preliminary rounds in the conflict but win the last one. That is what counts, for usually the last is the worst, the bitterest, and the hardest. Was this not true in the Gethsemane conflict? That was the devil's last throw or at least his last long attack.

But the devil never gives up the struggle while there is breath in us. In His last hours on earth, one of the two thieves crucified with Jesus challenged Him with the request, "If thou be Christ, save thyself and us." I remember a dear saint who had been a shining example of faith and prayer for years. Yet in her dying moments she was assailed with great doubts and fears and needed the strong consolations of other Christians as she "crossed the river."

Worthy of more than a passing thought are the battlegrounds of the first and last Adams in their temptations. Preceding the Fall, the first Adam had a perfect environment and failed in it; preceding the Cross, the last Adam had adverse conditions and triumphed in them. The first Adam had no hunger and everything was to his taste; the last Adam had hunger in a wilderness with wild beasts. Adam used a legal appetite for an illegal purpose. Who says that perfect environment will produce perfect men? A perfect man in a perfect environment can still fail—witness Adam; but a perfect Man in a very imperfect situation can triumph—witness Christ. The Saviour, who had a legal right to use His power to make bread, refused himself that right.

Everything that Adam needed for his happiness was in the Garden of Eden; nothing that the Lord needed was in the wilderness. In the Garden Adam walked with God; in the wilderness Jesus walked with the devil. Eden was unmarred beauty; the wilderness was unrelieved ugliness. In Eden Adam was tempted once, and he fell; in the wilderness Jesus was tempted in all points and never once fell. The Eden calamity of Adam was the prelude to the fall of the whole race;

in God's plan for the redemption of the whole race, the wilderness triumph was the first round of victory.

In the Garden of Eden the first Adam had a companion; in the wilderness Jesus was alone. In Eden the temptation was short in duration; in the wilderness the temptation was protracted. The wilderness presented an opportunity to test Christ first in the realm of the body—"He was afterward an hungred" (Matt. 4:2b). But Adam had not fasted. There was no hunger-ground in him for Satan to exploit. The Evil One attacked his mind and his will by the medium of the fruit. Adam yielded and so lost this contest with his adversary. He lost his dominion and became dominated. Adam satisfied self; Jesus refused to satisfy himself. Adam pleased the devil; Christ pleased the Father.

Adam's failure lost him the dominion over the world; Christ's victory established His right over it without Satan's offered short cut. Satan blinded Adam's eyes to the fact that in his one act of disobedience he was involving millions. But Satan could *not* seduce the thinking of the Son of God the same way. Maybe it was by reason of Adam's short-term thinking on the issues involved in the commitment to the devil's plan that he fell. Was one of the reasons for the extension of Christ's temptation His delayed action by reason of His long meditation over the issues? There can be no thought that the Master engaged the devil outside an atmosphere of intense prayer. The battle in the wilderness was not only for Christ to be in subjection to the devil, but for the devil to keep in perpetual bondage the whole human race, involving this writer and you, my dear reader.

No temptation has come your way that is too hard for flesh and blood to bear. But God can be trusted not to allow you to suffer any temptation beyond your powers of endurance. He will see to it that every temptation has a way out, so that it will never be impossible for you to bear it.

—I Corinthians 10:13 (Phillips)

And you can avoid falling; for, first, no temptation has overtaken you but such as man may well withstand; secondly, God is true to His promise: He will not allow you to be tempted beyond your power of resistance; nay, along with each temptation He will provide the door of escape, so that you may be able to endure.

—I Corinthians 10:13 (Way)

Chapter 7

SHAPED TO GOD'S DESIGN

When a see-it-all-in-a-glance tourist flitted through the priceless art treasures of the Louvre in Paris, she swept her critical eye over some of the world's greatest paintings. As she left the fabulous works of the great masters, she sniffed with disdain and said, "I don't think much of them." The gendarme replied coldly, "Madame, people do not judge these pictures; these pictures judge people." The newly-rich madame was stunned.

To the Word of God this same application might be given: we do not judge the Word; the Word judges us. No wise man will dismiss the Book of the Lord with a wave of the hand. That there are some things hard to be understood within its covers, none will deny. On the other hand, he who will seek the mind of the Spirit will certainly have an unveiling of the truth that the Spirit himself has written. Though the seeker be a wayfaring man and unlearned, he need not err therein. The Bible is not just a series of puzzles to be deciphered. It has a chain of commandments to be obeyed.

Yet in explaining the truth, who is to say, "So far shalt thou go and no further"? What determines interpretation? Can Bible truth be rejected or conveniently ignored because it is overdemanding upon us morally and materially? To cut this whole matter down to the irreducible minimum, perhaps we should ask this question: "Can the Bible standard of Christianity be lived today?" Again and again when some truth is discussed, one hears the statement: "But we are living in different days!" That is undeniably true. Do we then alter our interpretations of Bible truth to fit the days? Or should we alter our thinking to fit the Bible?

Just how do men come to spiritual maturity? It seems that failure to discover reality shows up to many only after they have spent their money for that which is not bread. So often their lament is "I wish I were younger and could start over again to serve the Lord." Certainly if money could now buy them out of their dilemma, they would give it. Some would barter all they have in order to get into the midstream of blessing and power. But because they have balked at the price God asked them to pay in Christian service, or because they were saved in life's later years, they have missed much of the blessing of earthly and eternal reward. Those lost years can never be reclaimed.

But here is what such people can do. In the first place, if they have not already received Christ in His fullness, they can repent of all sin, seek cleansing by the blood, and on the basis of Luke 11:13 ask the Holy Spirit to fill and flood them with himself. After this blessed experience of enduement, the next step is a discipline by the Spirit in all matters pertaining to body and soul.

It must be true to say that God never takes two believers to spiritual heights by the same path. God made all trees, but look at the difference in them. John the apostle may have been as great a saint as Paul. but John's service for the Master, though it must have been of the same quality as Paul's, was not of the same quantity.

There is no doubt at all that in the natural realm some people pay a greater price to enter the kingdom of God than do others. I have a friend whose father is a millionaire. When this splendid young man graduated from a famous college in America, the father offered to set him up in any business the youth chose. Here was a wide open door of material success offered to a full-blooded, eager youth. But my friend turned down the gracious offer from his father, saying, "Dad, I would rather serve God as a pastor of a church than do anything else in the world."

Or again, I think of a boy who came to Cliff College, England, with a glowing testimony. There was not a shade of self-pity about him nor the slightest color of boasting. Here is what had happened: His father had been very fond of him, and they were very close. They had shared sports and many other activities. Then came the parting of the ways, for when the boy was wonderfully saved, the father, angry that the son would not stand with him in the way of sinners, offered an ultimatum—quit religion or leave home. The son chose the latter, so the father dumped the boy's belongings outside the door and told him to go. The boy did just that—and did it in victory too.

When some people get saved, they have to give up cocktail-drinking friends, the country club, and the like. Some have to sell their shares in liquor investments. In ten thousand different ways the Spirit begins to make claims upon His own. But then after He has tried them, they come forth as gold. If I could write another beatitude, it would be this: "Blessed is the man who does not argue with the Spirit." In dealing with God we ought not to have a "Why?"

Make no mistake about it—some people do just this: argue with God. For if God says, "Do this," their first question is, "Why?" I thank God my father taught me that when he said a thing, he meant it for my good; therefore the "why" was not needed. Many believers wonder why the Lord lets the devil go as far as he does in trying their faith. Peter might easily have wondered the same thing. For instance, Jesus had said to him, "Satan hath desired to have you, that he may sift you as wheat," and then added, "but I have prayed for thee." Yet on other occasions Christ had cast out devils. "Why," Peter might have asked, "did Christ not drive the Evil One back to the region from whence he came?"

We too might ask, "Why did God let Satan experiment with Peter? What if Peter had cracked under this pressure?" The answer must be that Peter needed this testing and that right there the Master's prayer for Peter would be so effectual that he would come out in victory. If the question is asked, "Then why did Peter fail Jesus and deny Him?" I would say Peter failed because he got into the wrong company. He had to learn that in order to be made a rock he needed an upper-room experience. Moreover, the real work of the Master in Gethsemane was to pray himself through—and this He did.

Just what is God's goal in my life, and what is He after in me? What vessel am I to be, and what service shall I render Him? Taking a long-distance view, what is God fashioning out of my life for the millennial age and eternity?

Outside my window the pipe in the cold, snowy earth is continually carrying life-giving water to the school, although it gets neither recognition nor appreciation for it. Of course we would talk plenty if this hard frost and keen winter broke that pipe! Obviously the pipe ministry is hidden. Shall I too serve in a hidden ministry?

We have such childish ideas of God. A little girl said to her mother that she learned a new chorus at Sunday school. "What is it?" Mother asked. The wee one replied, "God is still on the phone." That mentality is not the child's alone, for some of God's children have that idea too. To them God is not much more than a great lawyer to get them out of all kinds of trouble, or else He is a great banker with endless gifts of money to supply all their needs.

But suppose we think of God in another way. He is a great artist, a great sculptor, shaping my life to His own design with a view to fitting me into His eternal program and making me "meet for the Master's use" both here and hereafter. If this, then, is the Lord's purpose and if His plan will not guarantee escape from suffering and inconvenience, shall I not be wise enough to expect experiences of temptations in all their unnamed varieties? Behind all of them is a God who "worketh all things after the counsel of his will." In the words of a Scripture verse (often twisted for our own ends), God is working all things together for good to them that love Him.

Gold tried in a fire is of greater value than gold which still has a mixture of alloys. Gold that is shaped into an ornament has yet more value. Of still higher worth is gold purified, then shaped into a vessel, and finally beautifully engraved.

Even so in a believer's life. The cleansed Christian—purged of all self-interest, self-glory, self-esteem, self-pity, self-projection—is of great value to God. Yet there is a maturity beyond this, eloquent in some by its presence, but conspicuous in others by its absence. A head stuffed with theology or even stuffed with Bible verses is no substitute for the deep things of God worked out in us by the Spirit. Mrs. Wesley, mother of the famous Charles and John Wesley, loved to repeat to them, "There are two things to do about the gospel—believe it and behave it." How right she was! How wise are they who both believe the gospel and behave it!

One of the lost arts these days is meditation. One would think that the slogan of many Christians is "There is a Book; who *runs* may read." On the contrary, we ought to be heeding the much-needed admonition, "*Take time* to be holy." In Part 1 of this book, we have been taking time to meditate on the subject of temptation. There are few of us indeed who, after our regeneration experience, have not been tempted to turn back for one reason or another. Few if any of us have not turned back somewhere. To have known any experience of backsliding, however severe or mild, is to have known something retrograde in the spiritual life.

Thank God that spiritual digressions need not be repeated. But just as man cannot leap over his own shadow, neither can he live without temptation. Perhaps we need to remind ourselves that ungodly people are also tempted, and that their capitulation in temptation is the explanation of wrecked homes, alcoholics, and jails.

In narrating the temptation of Jesus, Luke inserts a thought-provoking phrase of three words: "The devil departed from him *for a season*" (Luke 4:13). At a different time and in a different place and with different temptations the battle would be renewed, and for the same prize. At all costs Satan tried to divert Christ from the cross.

Satan's target is the same for us. I do not think Satan has fears about most Christians who are in the sinning-repenting cycle. Yet he has real reason to fear the man who is "dead indeed unto sin, but alive unto God." Such Christians will be tempted. But whatever the Christian's temptation, wherever it might be, whatever level it is on, there are definite guarantees from the Lord God omnipotent himself: first, that He "will not suffer you to be tempted above that ye are able"; second, that He "will with the temptation also make the way of escape"—the way of prayer and the way of the cross of Christ. The hymn writer says,

"I need Thee every hour,
Stay Thou near by;
Temptations lose their power
When Thou art nigh.

"I need Thee, O I need Thee,
Every hour I need Thee;
O bless me now. my Saviour,
I come to Thee."

THE TRANSFIGURATION

Six days later Jesus chose Peter, James and his brother John to accompany him high up on the hillside where they were quite alone. There his whole appearance changed before their eyes, his face shining like the sun and his clothes as white as light. Then Moses and Elijah were seen talking to Jesus.

"Lord," exclaimed Peter, "it is wonderful for us to be here! If you like, I could put up three shelters, one each for you and Moses and Elijah—"

But while he was still talking a bright cloud overshadowed them and a voice came out of the cloud: "This is my dearly loved Son in whom I am well pleased. Listen to him!"

When they heard this voice the disciples fell on their faces, overcome with fear. Then Jesus came up to them and touched them.

"Get up and don't be frightened," he said. And as they raised their eyes there was no one to be seen but Jesus himself.

On their way down the hillside Jesus warned them not to tell anyone about what they had seen until after the Son of Man had risen from the dead.

—Matthew 17:1–9 (Phillips)

PART II — THE TRANSFIGURATION

His whole appearance changed before their eyes, while his clothes became white, dazzling white—whiter than any earthly bleaching could make them.

—Mark 9:2b, 3 (Phillips)

In their presence he was transfigured, and his clothes glistened white, vivid white, such as no fuller on earth could bleach them.

—Mark 9:2, 3 (Moffatt)

INTRODUCTION

In the series of progressive crises that constituted the life of our Lord Jesus Christ, His transfiguration comes in for the least reference and comment. It is not mentioned in the Apostles' Creed nor, as far as I remember, in any of the other six creeds. Yet it is a vastly important turning point in the life of our blessed Lord. I am baffled at its omission not only from the six main creeds of the church but also from voices in the pulpits. In hearing preachers, famous and otherwise, in two hemispheres, only once have I heard a sermon on the subject of the Transfiguration of Jesus, and that by a student. Checking two volumes of sermons delivered at sundry times in many American pulpits by a great variety of theologians and preachers, I find not a single sermon on this stirring theme. Is this planned evasion? I think not—just sheer negligence, for this golden milestone in our Saviour's short ministry is worthy of the closest scrutiny and application.

God repeatedly bears witness in a sequence of threes. For instance, we read, "There are three that bear witness on earth and three in heaven." That the Gospels record the event of the Transfiguration three times is not without significance. They mention the names of the three men who were with Him—Peter, James, and John. They tell us that one of these three men wanted to build three tabernacles. Later they remind us that Peter, the most impetuous of the three, denied his Lord three times. The Transfiguration introduces the Saviour to the third part of His ministry. The three favored disciples were with Him on three special occasions, each time in the shadow of death: first, in the house of Jairus; next, at the Transfiguration; and finally, in the most sacred spot on earth prior to Calvary—Gethsemane.

In the life of our Lord we accept the transfiguration experience as real, and not as Tertullian remarks, "just a vision." Nor is it as old Mr. Meyer wants to tell us, "part vision and part objective reality." These disciples were no somnambulists. It does not help to believe the statement of that giant among Roman Catholic theologians, Thomas Aquinas, when he says that at the Transfiguration Moses borrowed a body for this manifestation. One wonders where the other fellow was while Moses borrowed his body.

Careful, complete doctrinal initiation has glued in our minds several points of our identification with Christ. The order goes like this:

Jesus was born of the Spirit; we too may be born of the Spirit.

He walked in the Spirit; we too may walk in the Spirit.

He was baptized in water; we too can be baptized in water.

He was victorious in temptation; we too can be victorious in temptation.

He died; we too can die to self.

He rose again from the dead; we too can have resurrection life.

He is seated at the right hand of the Father; we too are seated with Him.

Yet reflection carefully taken will reveal two outstanding experiences of the Saviour that we seldom if ever hear about as points of our identification with Him. The two notable omissions from this paralleling interpretation are His transfiguration and His Gethsemane. I wonder why in our teaching we so easily slip past or edge away from these major crises in the Master's life. Is it that the former, His transfiguration, was the introduction to a period of probation by deep suffering, and the latter, His Gethsemane experience, was the termination of it? This may well be the explanation.

Jesus certainly turned His back on the glories of heaven. The first time was at His birth, or as the theologians call it, His incarnation. Wesley says,

> He deigned in flesh to appear,
> Widest extremes to join,
> To bring our vileness near
> And make us all divine.

But on the Mount of Transfiguration Jesus turned His back a second time on the beckoning glory of the other world. At His incarnation He humbled himself to take our flesh; at His transfiguration, "being found in fashion as a man, he humbled himself [even to the humiliation of a malefactor], and became obedient unto death, even the death of the cross." His first baptism in water was a *public* initiation to a *public* ministry of service for others. The Transfiguration was a *private* baptism of glory for a *private* ministry of suffering. In both baptisms there was the manifestation of the audible voice of God. The Saviour rejoiced in that voice and walked in obedience to it. He proved what was "that good, and acceptable, and perfect, will of God."

Matthew's account makes it abundantly clear that for His personal encounter with God, the Saviour walked up the mountainside with the three favored disciples—Peter, James, and John. Those who trade in the popular religious cliché, "God has no favorites," will find it hard to explain their cheap interpretation in the light of Psalm 45:7: "Thou lovest righteousness, and hatest wickedness: therefore God . . . hath anointed thee with the oil of gladness *above thy fellows.*" I believe God always has had favorites, still does have favorites, and always will have favorites as long as there are men who live near to God's heart. In the journeyings through the wilderness, all Israel saw Moses go toward the rock at Rephidim, yet none but the elders could see Moses smite the rock. Likewise, Peter, James, and John learned Christ's secrets. They were often with Him in the crisis hours of His ministry. They moved in the inner circle of revelation.

At this point I beg you to pause and reflect this startling fact concerning the three men who saw the Transfiguration. These three amazed and amazing disciples, these who were eyewitnesses of Christ's majesty, these who heard of Christ's glory more than any other of the favored twelve, these who saw these things, who heard and knew the voice of God, who knew by name visitors from the regions beyond the grave—it was these men who soon backslid. Mark this fact well, for it is a stern warning. Glorious manifestations of divine power in lofty mountain ranges are not in themselves any guarantee of security against deflection and failure in the spiritual life.

We read the same warning in Christ's story of Lazarus and the rich man (Luke 16). In hell the rich man was shaken in his thinking and emotions. Lifting up his eyes, he cried to Father Abraham to send Lazarus to his five brothers so they could repent. To this Abraham replied, "Neither will they be persuaded though one rose from the dead."

I repeat: These three men on the Mount had visitors from eternity and more revelation than any other living man. Yet under the final assaults of doubt, they cracked. We have been warned.

And then, while he was praying, the whole appearance of his face changed and his clothes became white and dazzling.

—Luke 9:29 (Phillips)

While he was praying, the appearance of his face altered and his dress turned dazzling white.

—Luke 9:29 (Moffatt)

Chapter 8

TRANSFIGURED AS HE PRAYED

"After six days, Jesus . . . was transfigured." It would be easy just to slip past this simple introductory phrase without attempting to empty from it some of its meaning. But here, too, there is honey in the rock.

"After six days." Six days of what? First of all, they were days of secrecy. We read that it was when Jesus was praying *alone* that "his disciples were with him" (Luke 9:18). There is no hint of crowds.

Second, they were days of gloom, for the future was overcast with the shadow of death. Recently He had begun to show His disciples "how he must suffer many things . . . and be killed."

Third, they were days of stern sayings. To Peter, Jesus had just said, "Get thee behind me, Satan: thou art an offence unto me." That saying would be hard for Peter to take.

Fourth, Jesus' death offered the disciples themselves a dreary outlook, for He demanded their death too. His word to them was this: "If any man will come after me, let him deny himself. . . ," a commandment to Christ's disciples which has never been abrogated.

There is no clue that there were any miracles in these six days. There is no hint that eager crowds pressed upon Him for food or favors. Dr. G. Campbell Morgan in his *Crises of the Christ* expresses the passage this way:

> Those six days must have been among the saddest in the life of the Master: six days of silence, six days in which His loneliness was the supreme fact in His progress. He had chosen these men, but there was not one of their number who fully followed Him now. They loved Him, and He loved them, and "having loved them, He loved them unto the end." But the way to the end lay through desolate days in which He himself realized and they proved their present incapacity for fellowship with Him in suffering. He was moving in sublime loneliness to the cross.

From the transfiguration experience He is going down into the "valley of the shadow of death," but He will "fear no evil."

About three years earlier, the Son of God had undergone a fierce assault of forty days of temptation in the secret place of the wilderness. That episode is all but hidden from us. The darkness of those forty days is unillumined, save for three final attacks that the devil made upon Him. It was the Father in heaven who witnessed these forty days of warfare on the Master's soul, mind, and body. But He who saw in secret, rewarded Jesus openly a little later, for on the Mount of Transfiguration the Father delighted to honor the Son before men.

Concerning Christ's temptation and transfiguration in the wilderness, there is another contrast. After Jesus' earlier temptation experience, "angels came and ministered unto him" (Matt. 4:11). Again, toward the end of His life on earth, after the onslaught in Gethsemane, there came an angel from heaven to strengthen Him (Luke 22:43). But here in the transfiguration glory, there is a conspicuous absence of angels. Why? Because angels did not need to see His glory. At this time He did not need their attention. Doubtless had they been there, they would have repeated their act of veiling themselves before Him as they did in Isaiah's vision of the Son of God (Isa. 6:2; John 12:41). If the absence of angels at His transfiguration is startling to us, maybe it is equally surprising that Moses and Elijah have no wings! What strange appendages we have given the celestial people—wings and halos! At the Transfiguration, the Father's glory, bestowed upon the Son and shared with the Son, was the all-sufficient reward. What could be added to that?

Mere human words would be beggared to describe this majestic metamorphosis. The full current of this revelation is not conveyed by human phrases transferred onto thought waves. Here is a free translation:

> As Jesus ascended a mountain for prayer, He requested His three disciples, Peter, James and John, to accompany Him. While Jesus was thus engaged in prayer, His countenance appeared completely transformed. His face shone as the sun in its meridian glory. His garments became scintillating in their whiteness, beyond the purging whiteness of any earthly bleaching.

> Suddenly and silently Moses and Elijah appeared, robed in lesser grandeur, and speaking softly of Christ's coming death and departure at Jerusalem.
>
> At this awesome sight, Peter and his companions began to shake, though at length weariness subdued the three disciples into sleep. On waking they saw the glory sustained, with Moses and Elijah still standing beside Jesus.
>
> A radiant cloud then covered all three disciples. As they entered the cloud, fear gripped them. Coinciding with their fears, there came out from the midst of the cloud a majestic voice announcing, "This is my Son, My only begotten, in whom My soul delighteth. Hear ye Him."
>
> Hearing this utterance from heaven, the terrified disciples were prostrate with awe. Yet when Jesus stooped and touched them, He revived their hearts, saying, "Arise; fear not."
>
> Suddenly, as the three disciples turned around to look, Moses and Elijah, the two visitors, had disappeared; and Peter, James, and John were left standing alone, gazing at their Lord.

Just as one window inserted in a windowless room does wonders for the room, so one word inserted in Luke's version of the Transfiguration scene makes a world of difference, illuminating the story as well as our Lord's character. The one differentiating word that the other two evangelists who record the story overlook is the word *prayed* (Luke 9:29).

Prayer is the one word that is characteristic of Luke's entire interpretation of our Lord's life. All four evangelists say that as Jesus was being baptized, the Spirit like a dove descended upon Him; but it is Luke who adds the words: "Jesus also being baptized *and praying*" (Luke 3:21). Likewise, Matthew, Mark, and Luke all tell of the choosing of the Twelve, but Luke adds that it was after a night of prayer that Jesus elected them to office. In the story of the crucifixion it is Luke alone who mentions the prayer "Father, forgive them." Then, too, it is Luke who stamps the transfiguration story with the same word when he says, "*As he prayed*, the fashion of his countenance was altered." Jesus was transfigured while praying. The Greek word here interpreted as transfigured is *metamorphoomai*, which means "to change the form." Without question, the most transforming experience to life and vision is prayer.

Was Jesus always transfigured in the secret nights of prayer? It could be so. Prayer was His natural habitat. On the other hand, this occasion could have been the one and only time that He was so endowed with this other-world glory. Matthew and Mark's account of this change in Jesus differ from Luke's when they add the two words "before them." Jesus was transfigured "before them"—that is, in *their* presence. This was one time that men witnessed this magnificent metamorphosis.

In the book *The Mystic Way*, Evelyn Underhill says of Francis Assisi that when he was absorbed in prayer, he "became changed almost to another man." Once at least when praying by night and when "his hands were outstretched after the manner of a cross, his whole body was lifted up from the earth and wrapped in a shining cloud as though the wondrous illumination of the body was a witness to the wondrous enlightenment of the mind." Moreover, when St. Catherine of Bologna, always pale because of her chronic ill health, was emerging from communion with God, it is said that she was seen by her sisters "with shining rosy countenance radiant like light."

These experiences of Francis of Assisi and of St. Catherine are not equal with that of our Lord Jesus Christ, but they show the transforming power of prayer. There is no place on earth where one can shake off the dust of this world like that of the prayer closet. There is no place where the glory of God so impregnates the soul as the prayer closet, where we are still and know that He is God. The episode on the Mount of Transfiguration may have been the only night that Jesus was transfigured with the disciples witnessing the amazing event. Yet I am sure angels often saw Him transfigured as He sought a lonely spot for intercession night after night. I believe many of these nights were miniature Gethsemanes before the final onslaught in the Garden of Gethsemane.

Moreover there appeared to them Elijah accompanied by Moses; and the two were conversing with Jesus.

—Mark 9:4 (Weymouth)

And there appeared unto them Elias with Moses: and they were talking with Jesus.

—Mark 9:4 (King James)

Chapter 9

MOSES AND ELIJAH—
The Two Witnesses

God seems to love the figure three. We have three parts of the day—morning, noon, and night. We have land, sea, and water; past, present, and future; body, soul, and spirit. Men are colored black, yellow, and white. In the Trinity we have God the Father, God the Son, and God the Holy Ghost. The life of God's Son is divided into three parts: His childhood, His manhood (obscure and unrevealed), and His three final years of ministry as the Son of God to the sons of men.

Similarly, the scene on the Mount of Transfiguration offers us three studies. The first and foremost to attract our attention is the Son of God. The last deals with the actions of three onlookers—Peter, James, and John. The middle study we are about to consider concerns two visitors from the other world, for there talked with Jesus "two men who were Moses and Elias."

There were, then, five spectators of this transcendent spectacle. They say so little that I have a feeling we are only half informed. If we push too far in imagination, however, we shall be attempting to add perfume to the rose and thereby demonstrate mere folly.

How did the three disciples know these two witnesses were Moses and Elijah? Did the Lord Jesus call them by name? Surely they had been with Him in the "glory which [He] had with [the Father] before the world was." We do not know with real certainty how Moses and Elijah were identified. Sufficient for us that these men, Moses and Elijah, were rightly named.

In the fact that Moses and Elijah were recognized, we certainly have irrefutable evidence of the indestructibility of human personality. A modern scientist of great distinction, Dr. Wernher von Braun (whose name is inextricably involved with space-rocket research in the U.S.A.) has a timely word on this. I quote:

> Many people seem to feel that science has somehow made "religious ideas" untimely or old-fashioned. But I think science has a real surprise for the skeptics. Science, for instance, tells us that nothing in nature, not even in the tiniest particle, can disappear without a trace. Nature does not know extinction. All it knows is transformation. Now if God applies this fundamental principle of indestructibility to the most minute and insignificant parts of His universe, does it not make sense to assume that He applies it also to the human soul? I think it does. And everything science has taught me and continues to teach me strengthens my belief in the continuity of our spiritual existence after death. Nothing disappears without a trace (*Reader's Digest*, June 1960).

It is true that no comments from men confirm the Word of God, for God has established it for ever. Nevertheless, this extract is an interesting observation from a man who has emerged from the rubble of World War II after seeing his nation prostrated by it.

I *am* a spirit. I *have* a body. As wood may be burned and become gasses and ashes, my body may suffer the same end. But—and this is what matters—I *am* a spirit, and this spirit is indestructible. One can add, too, that after death the ego in its new manifestation is identifiable. We shall know as we are known. Dives *saw* Lazarus in the bosom of Abraham and *cried*, "Father Abraham, send Lazarus," clearly showing that he knew the one-time beggar who sat at his gate. On this transfiguration mount, Moses and Elijah are readily identified.

The whole transfiguration scene beggars words and flees before the artist's brush. Here is solemn language. Here is holy ground. The brief lifting of the veil for a moment in order that we might see the King in His beauty is mightily moving. One sometimes wishes Handel had given this transfiguration scene some place in his majestic oratorio *Messiah*. Was the chariot that whisked Elijah away years before again very near at hand to give a regal entry for the King of glory to enter heaven? If it were, He turned His back upon that beckoning relief. Did our Lord remember that Moses took a long walk and failed to return? Did He think that by this short cut to eternity He too could escape the gruesome path of suffering?

Speculative as this is, it must have been a path open to Him. Jesus knew the supreme will of the Father was that He should endure the cross, despise the shame, and gain the right hand of the Father in glory. Of all this, Moses and Elijah reassured Him, speaking of the death that He should accomplish in Jerusalem.

One title of the blessed Holy Spirit is the Comforter. In the early church Barnabas acquired the warm name of "son of consolation." Later on Paul speaks on this wise: "God comforteth those who are cast down" and "comforted us by the coming of Titus." Shall we assume here that Moses and Elijah were commissioned from the council chambers of eternity to comfort the Saviour as He took the first steps toward the exodus that He would accomplish at Jerusalem? Blessed ministry!

To the three favored men—Peter, James, and John—it must have seemed that the ages had been put into reverse and that history had caught up with them. As they turn from the blazing light of Christ's glorified body, they see the thrilling sight of two men from another world. Who said, "No one ever came back to tell us"? Two did, Moses and Elijah—not orally but by their presence. What astonishment must have taken hold of these two! Two at least were dumb with ecstasy at the glory of Christ. This must have been like a window into heaven! Speaking of this unmatched revelation, John wrote later, "We beheld his glory, the glory as of the only begotten of the Father, full of grace and truth."

And two men also were talking to Him, who were Moses and Elijah; who, appearing in magnificence, spoke of His departure, which He was about to celebrate at Jerusalem. Now Peter and those who were with him, had been heavy with sleep; but on being fully roused, they saw His majesty, and the two men standing with Him.

—Luke 9:30–32 (Fenton)

Chapter 10

WHY MOSES AND ELIJAH?

Why did God choose Moses and Elijah to witness the Transfiguration? The principle of divine selection is past finding out. In the Old Testament days there was an abundance of spiritual giants, and a host of men of indomitable courage, and a galaxy of heroes of faith. Millions had lived in those days. Who but God could select the correct escorts for Christ in the transfiguration majesty?

Out of the millions awaiting their final release into the full glory of heaven, why should God select Moses and Elijah to appear on the Mount of Transfiguration? Would not others also like to see the King in His beauty? Surely there were others with longings. At any rate, on their election to this sublime office, Moses and Elijah must have had ten thousand congratulations from other saints of that other world. (I wonder how the angels felt about their own omission from the scene.)

In answer to the question "Why Moses and Elijah?" we offer two suggestions. First, *Moses and Elijah were men of prayer*. Prayers never die. We read in Revelation 8:3 that there was given unto the angel much incense "that he should offer it with the prayers of all saints upon the golden altar which was before the throne." At Sinai Moses had cried, "Show me thy glory." This prayer of one of God's saints had been lodged beneath that golden altar for 1500 years. Yet now his desire to see God's glory was fulfilled to the letter on the Mount of Transfiguration. Moses, who had longed to enter the Promised Land, was at last on the mount in that land, with a manifestation beyond anything the Israelites had ever seen. He had esteemed the reproach of Christ "greater riches than the treasures of Egypt." He had rejected the lush court of Pharaoh for the complicated task of leading a despised and disgruntled people. Amid the soul pressure of this thankless chore, he had "endured as seeing him who is invisible." As a reward for obedience and 1500 years of patience, Moses' prayers were answered. Now he had a visible manifestation of Christ's glory. God is never in a hurry.

As I have said in my book *Why Revival Tarries,** "No man is greater than his prayer life." That the Almighty will condescend to lay hold of a man is wonderful. That this same holy and undefiled God will allow a man to lay hold of Him in prayer is more wonderful still, it seems to me. Moses was one such man who "stood . . . in the breach, to turn away [God's] wrath, lest he should destroy them." And when all others quit, it was Elijah who stood in the breach against the prophets of Baal.

At the time of the Transfiguration, the Son of God was about to stand in a gap too. The greatest revealed prayer battle—Gethsemane—loomed ahead for the One who was there praying and being transfigured on the

**Why Revival Tarries,* $2.00 *postpaid from Bethany Book Shop.*

Mount. Maybe at this junction there was quickened to Christ's holy mind the past history of Moses and Elijah. Surely Jesus himself would ask, "Why of all those in holy warfare are these two men in particular My companions on the Mount?"

Moses had stood alone against a rebellious and backslidden people and stolen a nation from the lash of God's anger, even when his companions failed him. On a hill called Carmel, Elijah had stood against the principalities and powers of a devil-inspired system. In like manner, Christ was soon to make the greatest single payment of all time—alone. In His own blood He was about to turn the anger of the Lord from those sinners who would accept His sacrifice. Soon on a hill called Calvary, the Christ of the Transfiguration would battle the hierarchy of hell. Though man-forsaken and God-forsaken, He would triumph gloriously and come to ultimate and unparalleled glory, a glory beyond that which Moses and Elijah shared on the Mount—as far beyond as that fireball in the heavens is beyond the pale and lifeless moon.

Secondly, *God chose men to appear on the Mount who were lonely men.* Loneliness is hard for most of us to take. We all like fellowship. The blare of radio, the incessant flashing of the TV, the gas-filled highways, the almost endless parade of breakfast and luncheon meetings (even with a Christian atmosphere)—all these witness the fevered temperature of us moderns in our attempt to escape loneliness.

Yes, Elijah and Moses were the products of the country and quiet places. Flowers do not grow on turnpikes, nor do springs flourish there. Retirement for the purpose of meditation is in divine order. The poet Isaac Watts says,

> What is the creature's skill or force,
> The sprightly man or warlike horse,
> The piercing wit, the active limb?
> All are too mean delights for Him.

Then he significantly adds,

> But saints are lovely in His sight,
> He views His children with delight;
> He sees their hope, He knows their fear,
> And looks, and loves His image there.

There are a thousand competitive claims against withdrawal for meditation. So often, and with great justification, it has been said that God employs the busy man. This is true. But it is equally within the facts to state that the Lord has pulled men from the furnace of duty to the solitudes. Witness Moses on Nebo or at Pisgah. After Aaron was allowed to go so far and no farther, God took Moses and wrapped him in a cloud so that others could not see him and he could not see them. Though, on the one hand loneliness can be very frightening, on the other hand it can be very inspiring.

When the Lord Jesus Christ had the company of these two nation-shaking men, Moses and Elijah, He might have had thoughts like these: Elijah and Moses were recluses first, and then they were rejects. But finally they were redeemers. To be patterned after Elijah and Moses, therefore, is to be first a recluse and then a reject. The memory of the courage and zeal of these two Old Testament men, as well as the knowledge that the Father had empowered them, would be fortifying to Jesus as He entered the rugged way to the rugged cross. He too was soon to suffer all that Moses and Elijah ever suffered, and more.

There is a distinct parallel between the life of Moses and the life of Jesus. Because of persecution, Moses had to be hidden by his mother at his birth; Jesus, too, had to be taken to Egypt for safety at the time of His birth. Moses lived to deliver Israel out of the bondage of Egypt; Jesus will deliver from the bondage of sin and the dominion of the devil all men who will trust Him. Moses smote the rock from which living water saved a nation; Christ is that Rock from whose smitten side flows a river of blood that will cleanse those who believe. As Wesley has said,

> Grace is flowing like a river;
> Millions there have been supplied;
> Still it flows as fresh as ever
> From the Saviour's wounded side.
> None need perish, none need perish;
> All may live, for Christ has died.

Elijah was a mystery, another Melchizedek. As far as the Bible record goes, Elijah was without father and without mother. Place and pedigree did not belong to him. Tiny Tim in Sunday school knows Elijah's end (where and how Elijah finally went). But how did Elijah come? Where did he train for his office? How old was he when he appeared first to King Ahab? How long was he in hiding until the day of his showing forth? We know not. John the Baptist was hidden for probably twenty years and then had only six months of ministry. But what a ministry! The Redeemer was hidden away from public ministry for twenty years too; then came the greatest ministry that man has ever seen. Surely God's ways are not our ways.

But why was Elijah chosen? Had intuitive knowledge been given to him that this Man Jesus Christ would make an offering of His own blood greater than that of all "the blood of beasts on Jewish altars slain"? Had there been given to Elijah (but hidden from us) a communication that this transfigured Man would one day bring fire down from heaven as he himself did on Carmel—a fire which will endue a church and revolutionize human personality? Jesus himself said, "I am come to bring fire on the earth" (Luke 12:49). Elijah's descending fire shattered the false priests of Baal. But the fire that the Lord would send would humble the might of Satan, burn out the superstition of the witch doctor, and unhinge the false security of the cultivated sophisticates in yonder university.

These two men, Moses and Elijah, knew what it meant to be wounded in the house of their friends, to be neglected by a whole nation; for Aaron failed Moses, and the prophets failed Elijah. At the Transfiguration Christ was heading for betrayal by friends and rejection by the nation. On the Mount with Him, we glimpse again these two triumphant men. The type of body they have is not mentioned, nor does it matter. They are perfectly at home. Neither of them says, "Why hast thou disquieted me to bring me up?" Here are "the spirits of just men made perfect," and soon they will return from whence they came. What a story they will have to tell those who for a millennium and more have cried, "How long, Lord, how long?"

Notice that Moses and Elijah had no animated discussion with Peter, James, and John about the other world. What unknown things they might have told us! What mysteries could have been illumined! But there was complete silence, or else a conversation not intended for our ears. After Paul's exalted experience in the heavens, he found it not lawful to utter the things that he had seen and heard.

Moses and Elijah were men of the mountains—and so was the Son of God. Moses and Elijah were betrayed spiritually by their next of kin—and this lot befell the only begotten Son of the Father too. Moses and Elijah were ordained to usher in new eras (Moses, that of the Law; Elijah, that of the prophet)—here is One who has the keys of the kingdom. He is stronger than Samson, wiser than Solomon, more patient than Job, and more courageous than Joshua. He it is who opens the greatest era known to men.

We can only guess about the thoughts that passed through the mind of the Son of God on the Mount of Transfiguration. But they must have dwelt partly on these chosen men, Moses and Elijah, and their part in the plan of God, as well as on God's complete faithfulness in bringing them to glory.

Just as they were parting from him, Peter said to Jesus: "Master, it is wonderful for us to be here! Let us put up three shelters—one for you, one for Moses and one for Elijah."
—Luke 9:33 (Phillips)

And when these were preparing to depart from Jesus, Peter said to Him, "Rabbi, we are thankful to you that we are here. Let us put up three tents—one for you, one for Moses, and one for Elijah."
—Luke 9:33 (Weymouth)

Chapter 11

PETER'S REQUEST

The bias of most commentators seems to be against Peter for his request "Let us make here three tabernacles." By many, there is a suggestion, or at least an inference, that Peter wanted to stay up there in the Mount to escape the drudgery of earthly ministry. This is purely a speculation! I think Peter's request was honorable, even delightful. What was wrong with wanting to stay longer in the presence of the eternal God, beholding the glory of God at least for a little while? That Peter's request was legitimate seems obvious enough from the fact that he prefaces it with "If thou wilt." He wants nothing outside the will of God. There is nothing wrong with that.

Did Peter have memories of the historic manifestation of the glory of the Lord that had once appeared in the tabernacle in the wilderness and also in the temple? Many and minute were the details for the building of the tabernacle in the wilderness. Lengths and breadths, colors and sockets, were all to be fitted according to the Lord's word to Moses, and specifications were given for the trimmings of pomegranates and bells of the priestly robes. But all these, as well as the intricate offering on the brazen altar, led to one place—the holy of holies. Within this most holy place there was but one piece of furniture—the ark of the testimony with its mercy seat and two cherubim. The remarkable thing about this area of the tabernacle was that it had no window, no golden candlestick, no natural or artificial light. Only the glory of the Lord could illumine its darkness. Thus we read: "Moses finished the work. *Then* . . . the glory of the Lord filled the tabernacle" (Ex. 40:33, 34).

Four hundred and eighty years after the children of Israel had left Egypt, Solomon began to build the most fabulous temple men ever devised. This labor of love took seven years. Solomon, the perfectionist, completed every detail in construction. The magnificent splendor of this house of the Lord was overwhelming. Listen to this:

> Solomon overlaid the house within with pure gold: and he made a partition by the chains of gold before the oracle; and he overlaid it with gold. And he overlaid the cherubims with gold. And the floor of the house he overlaid with gold, within and without. The doors, . . . the carvings, . . . and palm trees, . . . and overlaid them with gold. . . . And they brought up the ark . . . and the tabernacle of the congregation, and all the holy vessels (I Kings 6:21, 28, 30, 32; 8:4).

Here, then, are the details of this resplendent house of the Lord. It has the ark, the holy vessels, the cherubim, a carpet of gold on the floor, walls of gold, palm trees of gold, a host of priests. What did it lack? As far as man was concerned, it was complete. Nothing could be added by the cunning of men. But Solomon knew something was needed—the glory of the Lord. Moreover, he was in direct line for God to do His part because he himself had done everything according to the pattern given. And so,

> It came to pass, when the priests were come out of the holy place, that the cloud filled the house of the Lord, so that the priests could not stand to minister because of the cloud: for the glory of the Lord had filled the house of the Lord (I Kings 8:10, 11).

The glory that Christ had with the Father before the world was had descended like a cloud and filled Solomon's temple. What was the temple of gold without glory? It was as empty as an ornate and expensive china dinner plate is without food. Alas, alas, we Christians live in a day when few of us can remember times when the glory so descended that "the priests could not minister, and the saints shouted aloud for joy."

Back now to the Mount and to Peter's request to build three tabernacles. How often in the last three or four years had Peter gone to the temple worn out from being tempest-tossed in his little fishing boat on Gennesaret, and then asking for spiritual bread, had received only the stone of mere ritualism? How often had Peter heard Scriptures read in the temple concerning the glory of God appearing in Moses' tabernacle and Solomon's temple? I am sure the shell of the temple, long empty of its glory, had sickened Peter and mocked his yearnings.

But on the Mount of Transfiguration Peter was one of the privileged three who saw Christ's face shine as the sun. There was majesty! There was beauty! The glory of the Lord had arisen on the privileged three. Peter later called it "the excellent glory" (II Pet. 1:17).

Stephen, the first martyr of the Christian church, had the inner glory too. He was brought before the council and a charge proffered against him. Then this young saint was allowed to speak. God's imperishable record of this event stands thus:

> All that sat in the council, looking stedfastly on him, saw his face as it had been the face of an angel. And he said, . . . the God of glory appeared unto our father Abraham (Acts 6:15; 7:2).

Finally the account of Stephen closes:

> When they heard these things [the history of Israel], they were cut to the heart, and they gnashed on him with their teeth. But [and what a contrast!] he, being full of the Holy Ghost, looked up stedfastly into heaven, and *saw the glory of God, and Jesus* standing on the right hand of God (Acts 7:54, 55).

Stephen, too, had been transfigured!

The core of the glory on the Mount was the voice of God the Father. It was the voice that mattered. In most of our lives there have been times when we could sing from actual experience, "Visions of rapture now burst on my sight." But the anchor of the soul is when we can truthfully say, "The Lord said unto me." Perhaps this is an added reason why Peter wished to build a tabernacle on the Mount. He would like a place where, in the despairing hours of life, he could hear the voice as well as see the glory.

The fact is that no elaborate ritual and stained-glass windows with lofty music make up for the absence of the living presence of the Lord himself. In Jesus' boyhood when His parents journeyed back from their great camp meeting at Jerusalem, they were in the congregation of a joyful people who were singing psalms of deliverance. They had had a great time! Great was their joy. But—and here we have what I think is the most incredible thing in their lives—they lost Jesus. Mary and Joseph lost Jesus and (believe it or not) journeyed without Him for one whole day. Scripture puts it this way: "They, *supposing* him to have been in the company." But all their suppositions did not put Him there! He was miles back in Jerusalem. Mary and Joseph supposed that He was there, and He was not.

Mary Magdalene, on the other hand, supposed that He was not there, and He was there! On Easter morning Mary Magdalene saw a moving figure in the gray light of the morning and supposed Him to be the gardener. Yes, He was there, without any ornate building, without any incense, without any priests.

Today missionaries know that in the steaming jungle under dripping leaves, whenever two or three are gathered together in the Lord's name, He is there. But how far can we sometimes go—singing hymns, being orthodox, hating false cults, and keeping up spiritual appearances—without realizing that Christ is not in the midst? Today whenever the Lord's glory is not in His sanctuary, His voice is not heard. And so, despite our clever interpretations in the pulpit, the people, unfilled, turn again to the world.

No, I cannot feel Peter is to be blamed for wanting to build three tabernacles. We have twisted and tortured

Peter's words, and he has had the worst of the deal. Mark and Luke in their versions of this story imply that Peter was beside himself with the glory that he saw. Peter spake "not knowing what he said." This much is sure: the Lord did not rebuke him for his request. Then why should we?

But he [Peter] did not know what he was saying.

—Luke 9:33 (Phillips)

Chapter 12

NOT KNOWING WHAT HE SAID

When the three disciples saw Jesus' glory and the two men that stood with Him, Peter said, "Master, it is good for us to be here . . . not knowing what he said." But the voice of the Lord called Peter to a halt, for "while he thus spake, there came a cloud, and overshadowed them. . . . And there came a voice out of the cloud, saying, This is my beloved Son: hear him" (Luke 9:33–35). Because Peter was beside himself with the blessing of this abnormal and unique manifestation, he uttered something not lawful for him to utter.

How easy it is for us today to make vows, to swear fidelity to this, to join that, to make promises when the spiritual atmosphere or the emotional pull of a meeting is high—not knowing what we say. Many a believer has crippled his own arm of usefulness because of his unfulfilled vows. I can think of more than one man who has made "strong crying to God" for success and has "bargained" with Deity. If God would bless him in basket and in store and prosper his ways, then he in turn would tithe, give offerings to help finance missionaries, and the like. But when prosperity came, the brother found he had so many other commitments that he could not keep his promises.

This point is superbly illustrated from a factual case. An ambitious and gifted young man made a Jacob-like covenant with God: "If Thou wilt bless me, then I will unfailingly give Thee a tenth of my weekly income." He faithfully kept his vow, dividing his tenth between his church and some needy missionaries. Business boomed until finally his weekly pledge was over $500.

Five dollars a week had been easy to give. Fifty dollars was a delight. But five hundred dollars a week—that seemed an appalling sum! There were other places where the man could invest such an amount. There were also some additions that could well be made to his own house.

Finally the young man consulted his pastor. "Do you think," he asked, "that the Lord would mind if I gave half the amount to God? You see, it is such a lot to give every week that I have a struggle to hand it over."

The faithful pastor said, "I can see your point. I have never had a church member ask me a question like this before. I know one way out of the difficulty."

The young man's eyes brightened. "What is it?" he asked.

"I think," continued the pastor, "that we should ask the Lord to shrink your business, and then the tithe will be easier to give."

We had better not make vows if we know not what we say.

Sometimes Christian leaders emphasize their own opinions, not knowing what they say. I think of one leader who stressed a certain type of dress for those in fellowship with his group. He was inflexible in this thing, taking a cast-iron attitude and outlawing some ladies who would not conform. For years he held this pattern. Then the day came when his own daughter asserted her rights. His standard was not hers. There might easily have been a family rift and separation, except that under pressure the father backed down from his strong-willed offspring. When tested, the issue was found to be a matter of opinion and not a matter of conviction. The leader's action saddened some of his followers.

I think of another preacher who insisted that believers could not wear wedding rings. More than once he clubbed an audience with this teaching and harried to the altar some of the younger folk, penitent because they had "slipped" here. Later, this same leader went to another country where I happened to be living. There, believers do wear rings. The zealous preacher, who would tear an American audience apart on this issue of rings, which to him "divided the sheep from the goats," was completely silent on the matter in that foreign country. Because it was a custom there to wear a wedding ring, in the interest of "wisdom" he never uttered a word. Are there different standards for different countries?

I am not arguing the point about a ring or about any other private interpretation. What matters is this: When pressure comes from one's home circle, long-held standards are often dropped. It causes great grief to those who have hewed to the line for years, to find a leader or teacher so easily moved because of opposition or persecution. As long as teachers are consistent throughout, I am all for their holding private views on rings or plain and "unworldly weddings," or never buying new furniture or new clothes. But all too often they preach these things "not knowing what [they] said."

Let any younger folk who read this chapter be careful about making vows and resolutions that will be binding and hurting if their fulfillment is to be completed. I do not say you should not make vows. I do say first count the cost, then write out what you have committed yourself to and read it at least once a week. Many great souls in the work of the Lord have made resolves in early years and kept them consistently right through their life with little if any alteration. But to keep to the course the Lord has plotted and to finish the course with joy, a believer needs to wear the harness of discipline and know what he says. A train must have a track to run on or else its usefulness is destroyed. Peter knew not what he said on the Mount of Transfiguration. Our words have too often exceeded our wisdom.

We so often forget the things that we say in the tense moments of the soul. But these things are of such a nature that other people remember them. This is a smarting thing. Others charge us with hypocrisy or insincerity when there is a contradiction between our preaching and talk and our conduct. What a hurt the tongue has done, not by willful slander but by careless vows built without a foundation of conviction, and later abrogated by the conduct of the enthusiast who committed himself so insincerely. What a hurt to the body of Christ! One could write a volume on such hurts. Consistency, thou art a rare gem! My soul, take thy warning.

But while he was thus speaking, there came a cloud which spread over them; and they were awe-struck as they entered the cloud. Then there came a voice from within the cloud: "This is My Son, My chosen One: listen to Him."

—Luke 9:34, 35 (Weymouth)

Chapter 13

THE TESTIMONY OF GOD THE FATHER

Just before His majestic transfiguration at Caesarea Philippi, Jesus had queried the disciples concerning men's opinion of Him: "Whom do men say that I the Son of man am?" (Matt. 16:13). Four comments classified Jesus with the greatest of their prophets. One said Jesus was Elijah, thus comparing Him to the Old Testament prophet who called the nation back to God. Another said Jesus was John the Baptist, comparing the fiery indignation of the Son of God to John, that stern man of the desert, who thundered against the gross iniquity of the land.

Yet others likened Jesus to Jeremiah. Had men seen the Son of God so weeping over Jerusalem that in His sobbing voice they heard the echo of the weeping prophet? Jeremiah's mighty, heartbroken lamentation was this: "Oh that my head were waters, and mine eyes a fountain of tears, that I might weep day and night for the slain of the daughter of my people!"

Furthermore, some likened Jesus to "one of the prophets." This they said because if they could not compare Jesus with a particular prophet, they at least knew He bore authority from God.

After these four answers to Jesus' query, Peter gave his inspired answer: "Thou art the Christ, the Son of the living God."

But the capstone on this building of Scripture truth concerning who Jesus is came on the Mount of Transfiguration from the shadow of the overhanging cloud. It was the voice of the Father who said, "This is my . . . Son, in whom I am well pleased."

At Philippi, the discerning voices of those who called Jesus a prophet would be a comfort to Him. The voice of Peter, "Thou art the Christ, the Son of the living God," would be a tonic to Him. But it was the voice of the Father, made known from the cloud of glory on the Mount, that was a stimulant for the final scene in the gathering storm. This bolstered up Him who so soon would lead captivity captive and bring many sons to glory. What a consolation to the Son that voice must have been! What a confirmation to Peter! What a revelation to Moses and Elijah! From the Father's mouth came the supreme testimony of His love for His Son and also His pleasure in Him. These words would be invaluable undergirding for the Son's rough and deserted pathway ahead.

There were two other voices on the Mount, voices of heavenly messengers, for "there talked with [Jesus] two men, which were Moses and Elias: who appeared in glory, and spake of his decease which he should accomplish at Jerusalem." These two were not interpreters explaining Christ's death but messengers bearing news of that death.

Would it be wrong to say that Jesus was eager for this death? Was the Moses-Elijah conversation a recapitulation of man's failure from Eden until then? Before this the Saviour had known anger at the pigeon sellers and money-changers in their unblushing greed and defiling of the temple. As Jesus now thought of the octopus grip the devil had upon man and the upset of God's original plan for man, did He become incensed and hot with holy anger? (Holy anger is pure anger, white-hot.) Was He in a hurry to be avenged of His (and our) adversary, the devil? He was now setting His face toward the final goal—redemption for mankind from the curse of the law by becoming a ransom for sin. Did He thrill to know that He alone could and would, as Te Deum says, "overcome the sharpness of death and open the kingdom of God to all believers"? Was it not His unspeakable joy to know that "as in Adam all die, even so in Christ [the last Adam] shall all be made alive"? Was He not elated to think that thousands of saints in Abraham's bosom, plus Abraham himself with Enoch and a multitude which no man could number, were awaiting their release through His death and resurrection?

Did the Father's words cause Moses to recall hearing the voice from the midst of the burning bush? Did Moses now understand that as that experience had marked a major crisis in his own life, so God, speaking from the cloud, meant a new turn in the Son's ministry? The voice Moses heard from the midst of the bush was Christ's. But now Moses hears the Father's voice as He testifies of Jesus: "This is my . . . *Son*," and as He tutored the disciples, "Hear ye him."

Elijah had escaped the grim experience of death. Did he himself marvel that the Son must pass through death's icy and black waters? The death of Moses, on the other hand, had been secret, witnessed by God and perhaps by the angels. As Elijah and Moses spoke of the betrayal and public hanging of the Son of God, was Jesus himself stunned? We do not know. Scripture is silent about the conversation, mentioning only the theme of their talk, "his decease." How much did Elijah and Moses talk? How much, if at all, did Jesus talk? Were all these on the Mount of Transfiguration just one day? Who can tell? We only know from Luke 9:37 that "on the next day . . . they were come down from the hill."

The posture of Peter, James, and John at this particular time of the Transfiguration is noteworthy. "When the disciples heard it, they fell on their faces and were sore afraid." Well they might be afraid. It is beyond our knowledge how they stood this revelation of His glory while they were yet in the body of humiliation. Many years later on Patmos, John saw the Christ of God, majestic in glory; "his head and his hairs were white like wool, as white as snow; and his eyes were as a flame of fire; . . . his countenance was as the sun shineth in his strength." Note John's reaction: "I fell at his feet as dead." John was felled by the revealed glory of Christ. To John on the island of Patmos, God testified in the majesty of His resurrection glory. To Peter it was by His voice that the transfiguration glory was remembered.

At the time Peter betrayed Jesus his Lord, he apparently forgot this revelation of glory. But later Peter wrote about it, for its revelation had been a sheet anchor to his faith. Just why he remembered the Transfiguration, we do not know. Whether others were propagating false doctrines, or whether there was a severe attack by the devil upon his own heart, we are not told. But in some such experience Peter asserts concerning the Transfiguration:

> We have not followed cunningly devised fables, when we made known unto you the power and coming of our Lord Jesus Christ, but were eyewitnesses of his majesty. For he received from God the Father honour and glory, when *there came such a voice to him* from the excellent glory, This is my beloved Son, in whom I am well pleased. And *this voice which came from heaven we heard*, when we were with him in the holy mount (II Pet. 1:16–18).

Twice in these verses Peter mentions the voice.

The Apostle John also remembered the glory. He wrote in his Gospel: "The Word was made flesh and dwelt among us (*and we beheld his glory*, the glory as of the only begotten of the Father,) full of grace and truth" (John 1:14). The words in the parenthesis—"we beheld his glory"—must have been directed to the transfiguration scene. That was the glory that awed angels and seraphim so that before its blazing splendor, they hid their faces.

From Luke's account it would seem that the voice of Christ was not heard at all during the transfiguration experience. Luke simply says that "as he prayed, the fashion of his countenance was altered." Whether the Son articulated this prayer, we do not know. Even if He prayed out loud "with strong crying and tears," yet it would appear that the Father's later divine command to the disciples, "This is my beloved Son: *hear him*," was referring to something else. What then were the disciples to hear and when?

The disciples "heard" Moses and the prophets in the writing of the Old Testament. Jesus once said, "Ye have *heard* it said. . . ." The meaning is clear: Those who read what the prophets said "heard."

But what else did the Father expect the disciples to hear? They were soon to hear Christ speak of His resurrection before false witnesses, scribes, and elders, and before the withering scorn of Caiaphas. These said, "This fellow said, I am able to destroy the temple of God, and to build it in three days." One thing that the disciples must "hear" and believe is His resurrection.

Again, the disciples shall yet hear Him say as an anchor to their souls: "Hereafter shall ye see the Son of man sitting on the right hand of power, and coming in the clouds of heaven." They must give heed with diligence to Christ's "I will come again" (John 14:3).

On the night before Calvary they also were to hear some of the greatest words uttered from Christ's lips (recorded in John's Gospel, chapters 14–17). At that time they were to hear the truth of their union with Christ clearly portrayed in the Master's masterly picture, "I am the vine, ye are the branches." In addition, they were still to listen with breath-taking wonder to the longest recorded prayer of the Saviour (John 17). That prayer, the old Puritan preacher of the 17th century, Thomas Manton, called "the dying blaze of Jesus."

If our Lord gave an exhortation to the disciples right on the Mount, then it is unrecorded. As I have inferred, it might well be that the Father was saying, "Having ears, hear what my Son will say before His decease, of which Moses and Elijah have spoken."

The final teachings of Jesus, then, were to be as anchors to hold them from shipwreck during the Gethsemane-Calvary days. Alas, they forgot them!

In his second epistle, Peter urged others to accept the three disciples' view: "We have also a more sure word of prophecy; whereunto ye [to whom I am writing] do well that ye take heed." Did Peter remember at that time that in the hour of his temptation he had forgotten Jesus' own sure word of prophecy to him? Would he now save others the failure that he himself had known? We believe so.

Peter's word is for us too, "upon whom the ends of this age have come." We are to take heed. We too must "hear him." These are days of seducing spirits and doctrines of devils. A skilled navigator at sea does not follow scurrying clouds however artistic they may look. Neither does he follow the wake of another vessel. He takes his bearings by things that are fixed—by the lighthouse, the stars, and the compass points. Even so, Scripture tells us to *take heed* to this "sure word of prophecy . . . as unto a light that shineth in a dark place."

Three disciples, then, as well as Moses and Elijah, were permitted to see on the Mount the crowning of the perfect Prophet. From there Jesus went down to Mount Calvary, then on to Mount Olivet with an undeviating course, with undivided attention, and with an unalterable determination to do the will of His Father.

A cloud also came, overshadowing them; and a voice came out of the cloud: "This is My Son, My Beloved: listen to Him!"

—Mark 9:7 (Fenton)

Then there came a cloud spreading over them, and a voice issued from the cloud, "This is my Son, the Beloved: listen to Him."

—Mark 9:7 (Weymouth)

Chapter 14

THIS IS MY BELOVED SON

I have never forgotten the cryptic analysis that a good Christian friend of mine made about William Temple, Archbishop of Canterbury—that distinguished scholar and Church of England leader. His terse comment was this: "William Temple was a man of foresight and also of insight."

Not many of us are blest with both foresight and insight. By our lack of these graces, we miss much. We can overlook, for instance, the combination of circumstances surrounding the story of Abraham's offering up of his only son Isaac. One relevant point of the story is the oft-overlooked suffering of the old father, Abraham, then about 113 years of age. From the moment that God challenged him to scale Moriah and there offer his only son Isaac, Abraham suffered a thousand deaths. There were at least three weary days and nights of this torture. Even the night before Abraham bound his son-offering on the altar, as the moon played its light on the tents and as Abraham looked at his lovely, innocent, sleeping son, he must have felt the cold steel of the dagger piercing his own heart.

Moreover, our guess is that the lad himself had not the slightest inclination that *he* was to be offered as a living sacrifice.

Similarly, today men often lack foresight and insight concerning the life of Christ. At what age Jesus Christ the Son of God became aware that He was to be offered a ransom for many, we do not know, though there have been many guesses. This we do know: For thirty-three years—from the moment that the Son left the ivory palaces for "this world of woe" (as Barraclough terms it)—the Father suffered. By the deep affinity of spirit between them, we are assured that every heart throb of the Son echoed in the heart of the Father. In the wilderness temptations, every blast the enemy gave upon the Son's tender spirit, every slight the Pharisees gave Him, every gibe the Sadducees thrust at Him—all these pained the heart of the eternal God, His Father.

This beloved Son, who is the delight of the Father's heart, is the Prophet among all prophets, the predicted Prophet among Old Testament prophets. He is the "Desire of the nations." In His ministry, Jesus was the Prophet from His baptism in the Jordan at the hands of John the Baptist until His transfiguration. After the Transfiguration He took the ministry of the Priest. Therefore it was at the event of the Transfiguration that Jesus "graduated" in what might be called the lesser events in His majestic life.

How did the Transfiguration affect the Father? It did affect Him, I am sure, and affected Him profoundly. (The Father's delight was that His beloved Son had done His will.) His voice declared, "This is my beloved Son, in whom I am well pleased."

Let us draw aside now and try in our limited way to grasp a fragmentary conception of the delight of the Father in His beloved Son at this time. In this age of scientific marvel, men can weigh the earth, take the temperature of the sun, fling a gadget-packed satellite into the air. But in other worlds, man's impotence is still spelled in capital letters. For instance, man is absolutely unable to span the greatest gulf known to man—the gulf between the holiness of God and the sinfulness of man. Oh sublime wonder—it was bridged by a Babe!

That Babe was independent of a human father in His birth, but He must be suckled by a human mother. The dimpled hand of that Babe would one day carry a nail on which the weight of the world's sin would hang. His baby hand that clutched a straw will in the future hold the seven stars of the book of the Revelation. That infant of days is the Ancient of days. That impotent Babe is the Lord God omnipotent. That gurgling baby-voice will one day be more majestic than an organ, for it will yet prove to be the "voice as the sound of many waters." That little baby head, so lacking knowledge and lying on its straw pallet, will one day reveal its omniscience. That Babe, before whom only a few nonfamous people bow and who is worshipped by nameless shepherds, will one day be manifest as the "great shepherd of the sheep."

At the manger no kings bow before Him—but before a hundred million angels, plus thousands of thousands, He shall yet be heralded as the "King of kings, and Lord of lords." He who was ushered into the world so quietly and with no other acclamation than that of angels which only a few witnessed, shall be acclaimed one day before all the living and before the raised dead. Amid a spectacle of glory that infinitely exceeds the utmost stretch of human conception, He shall one day have homage from every blood-washed soldier killed on battlefields of earth, from every last lost sailor, from lonely Mallory with snow for his shroud on the lonely heights of Everest, and every miner locked in his long tomb by that mine disaster—from all these, plus "all the kings of the earth and the great men, and the rich men, and the chief captains, and the mighty men, and every bondman, and every free man."

Having taken this lengthy aside, have we now grasped the Father's delight that His Son is half way to His goal of kingship? No wonder "there came a voice saying, This is my beloved Son: hear him."

In our gospel accounts of the magnificent spectacle of the Transfiguration, do we have a full report? Have we the complete record of the conversations that were made on this fascinating mount? Were the three disciples veiled from a part of this event and allowed to see and hear only that part where Moses and Elijah spake of His decease and the Father spake the thrilling word of benediction to the Son? Did the Father say more to the Son on this occasion than we have record of? "The great day" alone can answer these questions. At least they offer us some food for profitable thought.

We were not following a cleverly written-up story when we told you about the power and coming of our Lord Jesus Christ—we actually saw his majesty with our own eyes.

He received honour and glory from God the Father himself when that voice said to him, out of the sublime glory of Heaven, "This is my beloved Son, in whom I am well pleased."

We actually heard that voice speaking from Heaven while we were with him on the sacred mountain.

—II Peter 1:16–18 (Phillips)

Chapter 15

The Transfiguration— ITS MEANING TO CHRIST

Among Christians there is a baptism by water, and we have made much of that. There is also a baptism by fire, and to some degree we have stated that. But after the transfiguration of a life with a baptism of glory, there is another baptism about which we are almost silent. Six months before the crucifixion, Jesus said to the disciples, "Are ye able to drink of the cup that I shall drink of, and to be baptized with the baptism [of suffering]?"

From the mountain heights of the Transfiguration, the holy, harmless, and undefiled Son of God went down into a sea of suffering. From the glory He went down to the gloom. From the unspeakable joy of hearing His Father pass a vote of confidence and approval on all His work until that time, Jesus went on to the staggering isolation caused by the poor, defecting disciples in the Garden and in the trial, on to the final exasperation of a silent God!

Christ's glory-baptism on the Mount must have been a special means of ministry for His soul's fortification. This was the entrance to a future, gloomy tunnel of soul-strain that led to the waste places of the valley of humiliation. It was a special anointing for service. It was so in the Old Testament priesthood. By right of birth, sons born to Aaron were priests; but until they were anointed, they were not allowed to minister. Christ had this glory-baptism, this unique anointing of majesty on the Mount of Transfiguration. It was a gateway through which He began to tread the Via Dolorosa—the road paved with thorns and with the wicked devices of the unscrupulous men—the way that led to spirit pressure that no other man was ever called to endure—and the way to the glory-cross, reached through the Garden (a nom de plume for a battlefield). One Man was soon to combat legions of fiery hosts. This greater-than-Samson was about to prevail against the gates of hell. This greater-than-Solomon would soon manifest wisdom that would outwit the arch-schemer of the infernal kingdom. Every step from His mountaintop experience of the Transfiguration was down, until He was "lifted up." Well did Miss E. C. Clephane state it when she said:

> But none of the ransomed ever knew
> How deep were the waters crossed,
> Nor how dark was the night that the Lord
> passed through
> Ere He found the sheep that was lost.

After the Transfiguration all roads led to Gethsemane. His was the way of loneliness and loathing—loathing because to the pure One, everything mixed in that cup was impure. Did the memory of this blessed baptism of glory on the mountain return to the thinking of Jesus? Was this memory a mighty stabilizing power when the battle so surged over His soul later on in Gethsemane's grim darkness that He cried, "All thy billows are gone over me"?

Perhaps, too, that other word of the Father came to Him on that Mount of Transfiguration:

> Behold, I have given him for a witness to the people, a leader and commander to the people. Behold, thou shalt call a nation that thou knowest not, and nations that knew not thee shall run unto thee because of the Lord thy God, and for the Holy One of Israel; for he hath glorified thee (Isa. 55:4, 5).

It was on the Mount that the Father glorified the Son. Now on the Cross the Son will glorify the Father. "Ought not Christ to have suffered these things, and to enter into his glory?" (Luke 24:36).

But all of us who are Christians have no veils on our faces, but reflect like mirrors the glory of the Lord. We are transfigured by the Spirit of the Lord in ever-increasing splendour into his own image.

—II Corinthians 3:18 (Phillips)

All of us, with face unveiled
Gazing on the mirrored glory of our Lord,
Are hourly being transformed into the same likeness,
From a mere reflected glory into an inherent glory,
As may well be, since it proceeds from the Lord, the Spirit.

—II Corinthians 3:18 (Way)

Chapter 16

The Transfiguration—ITS MEANING TO US

Christ's experience of the Transfiguration was a pre-resurrection one. *Our* transfiguration must also be *before* our resurrection from the dead if we hold faithfully to our method of parallel interpretation:

He walked in the Spirit; we too may walk in the Spirit.
He was transfigured; we too can be transfigured.
He died; we too can die to self.
He rose; we too can rise to newness of life.

W. E. McCumber in *Holiness in the Prayers of St. Paul* says: "The prayer for entire sanctification . . . is after we find peace with God and before we go to meet Christ; it is after spiritual birth and before physical death; it is after we are justified and before we are glorified. In short, it may be now." This also is true of our personal transfiguration.

Our transfiguration is expressed by Paul in Romans 12:1, 2:

> I beseech you therefore, brethren, by the mercies of God, that ye present your bodies a living sacrifice, holy, acceptable unto God, which

> is your reasonable service. And be not conformed to this world; but *be ye transformed* by the renewing of your mind, that ye may prove what is that good, and acceptable, and perfect, will of God.

The word *transformed* is the same Greek word *metamorphoomia* that in Matthew is translated *transfigured*. The only other time it is used in the New Testament is in II Corinthians 3:18, where it is translated *changed*. To be transfigured or transformed is to be "changed into the same image from glory to glory." When a believer has an unassailable assurance that he is born again of the Spirit of God, he who has borne the image of the earthly now desires to bear the image of the heavenly. The normal sign of every Spirit-born soul is an aspiration after what Paul would call true holiness.

Who can doubt that there are false and weird versions of the life that is hid with Christ in God? The doctrine of Bible holiness has often suffered more from its exponents than from its opponents. Here is what might be a classic example of this distortion.

A doctor friend of mine served for years in Africa. In the course of his sojourn, he took many pictures of the raw life in which these benighted folk have fermented for years because of the church's unpardonable sloth. The slides he showed were untouched, the scenes provocative. After these eye-opening things had been flashed on the screen and the uninhibited life of these nationals revealed, a lady came to the doctor like a sleuth. She was disgusted, plus. Didn't he know that——? Yes, he did know.

"But, lady, you see this was——." He was cut off.

"The pictures are not fit to be shown," she violently protested.

He tried to reason with her again. He knew, like other promoters, that his pictures might be thought indecent. Sure, the natives were almost destitute of clothing. But the astonishing thing was that it was not their near-nakedness which appalled her. It was not the fact that they had brutal, inhuman methods of initiating their children into maturity. It was not that they were repulsive in their filth and abhorrent in their drunken brawls. His pictures conveying their savagery, as well as his talk about the base tribal rituals, had not moved her at all. She was grief-stricken because the lady missionary standing with the blacks wore a dress with only half sleeves! In her fetish-like attachment to externals, the dear soul had lost sight of the eternal and the infernal. Dress had gotten in the way of duty. Alas, how we can get blind spots on our spiritual eyes!

Again we say that when we come to deal with glorious truths of a Spirit-transfigured life, the doctrines of men have gotten in the way. That we hold the truth of a doctrinal outline on holiness is not the point. The acid test is this: Is the life transfigured? Is it conformed to the world or transformed by the renewing of the mind?

Think of the issue of dress again. From long experience with people who walk with God, I am sure Christians will be modest in their apparel. (Usually this is slanted at the ladies.) But while the absence of modesty is to be deplored, its presence does not in itself mean one is established in holiness. Witness that nun going down the street with her floor-sweeping dress.

Does that attire mean she is sanctified? Other points could be made here, but enough. We are persuaded that "the king's daughter" who "is all glorious within" will also be modest without. She will watch the length of her tongue as well as the length of her dress. She will be transformed, changed into the image of Christ.

We hold that in the King James Version the stately Elizabethan English word *transfigured* ("he was transfigured before them"—Matt. 17:2) means the same as the present usage of the word *transformed*. Conversely, the word *transformed* in the King James Version means *transfigured*. "Be not conformed to this world: but be ye [transfigured] by the renewing of your mind."

In II Corinthians 11:13, 14 the word occurs again:

> False apostles, deceitful workers, *transforming* themselves into the apostles of Christ. And no marvel; for Satan himself is *transformed* into an angel of light.

Present-day scholars, with the emphasis on re-focusing the words of the King James Version, have translated this word *transformed* (Greek *metamorphoomia*) not as "changed" but as "masquerade." The *Amplified New Testament* and Arthur S. Way in *Letters of St. Paul and Hebrews* so translate it. But the word *masquerade* means "to put on some external dress in order to deceive," "to put on a mask." Masquerading is what Satan did. Jesus never masqueraded. Satan as an angel of light can wear a cloak and masquerade so as to deceive the unwary, but he can never transform. He can never fulfill the deepest meaning of the word transform, which is "to change character."

In Romans 12 the Apostle Paul admonished, "Be *not* conformed to this world." Here he is reminding us that the true believer is not walking "according to the course of this world." Paul would say, "Beware of many adversaries. Beware of a subtle mesmerism from a world that fights to regain its lost hold upon the believer." The negative side of our transfiguration is "Be not conformed to this world."

But the positive side is this: "Be ye transformed by the renewing of your mind" (Rom. 12:2). In the earlier chapters of Romans, Paul gives a showdown of the lusts of the flesh, of the devil's ways with men, and of the human race (and Israel's glory too) lost because of sin. Then Paul shows God's plan of saving the lost world. Chapter 7 of Romans has been called the graveyard of theologians, the battleground of conflicting theologies. Its issue is this: Can Christians live transformed lives?

I once heard a world-famous preacher in Manchester, England, who in his own masterly way took us into the intricacies of the results of Adam's transgression, and showed the involvement of the whole race from that retrograde step. Then he expostulated on the whole recovery of man at great length and with astounding Biblical and theological skill. Whatever the first Adam had done, Christ had an answer for. He agreed with Newman when he said:

O loving wisdom of our God!
When all was sin and shame,
A second Adam to the fight
And to the rescue came.

O wisest Love, that flesh and blood,
Which did in Adam fail,

Should strive afresh against the foe,
Should strive and should prevail.

One would think that on the basis of God's omnipotence alone, theologians would be agreed that God is almighty and therefore able to deliver from *all* sin. But that theory of almightiness seems to be leaky when we deal with the problem of cleansing from sin and victory over it.

We could call a host of witnesses to bear testimony that they had trouble with the slime pit within them after they were born of God. Few theologians and Bible teachers argue the fact that after conversion something is needed. The battle concerns whether that slough of despond in the human heart *can* be cleaned out or not, or, to change the figure, whether or not this inner wretchedness "leads us by the nose" right to the grave. The blunt language in which many preachers and teachers think but do not express so crudely is this: "Christ is only a partial Saviour." Such men speak as if the grave had magic qualities. They find a safety valve for much of their substandard Christian living in the fact that Dr. So-and-So agrees. To them, that is the end of all wisdom. The plain fact is that just as Adam hid from the presence of God, so men try to find some branch of learning behind which to hide the piercing revelation of God's holy Word.

In the Old Testament days God's problem was not the Girgashites nor the Amorites nor the Canaanites. God's problem was the Israelites, His very own people. I am sure His problem today, too, is His own people. Why is so much of our Christianity unattractive? Are we really deeply concerned that we have untransfigured lives?

Transfiguration, we believe, is both a crisis and a process. There can be a known experience with Jesus Christ in crucifixion. Romans 6:7 says, "He that is dead is freed from sin." Again, Paul says in Colossians 3:3, "Ye are dead, and your life is hid with Christ in God." Paul is here speaking to once-dead men who were now alive—yes, and more alive than those who boast of life. Regeneration is a birth; sanctification, on the other hand, is a death. There is a fashionable escapist theology abroad. Ruskin said many years ago that we want to go *to* the Cross, but few want to get *on* the Cross. We want Christ to die *for us*, but we do not want to die *with Him*. Christianity is all right if I can use it to my own ends. But when Christ wants to purge my squirming ego, crucify my stubborn self-will, seek to eliminate my reeking self-pity, vanquish my vacillation, and claim to reign supreme within the heart that He has purged—that is another matter.

A minister, whose degrees were strung behind him like the tail of a kite, protested with a little heat that my picture of the believer's entering into Christ and of Christ's entering into the believer was overdrawn and therefore confusing. I listened carefully to him. He was sure that while we are in this body, the Christian life oscillates between victory and defeat. He embraced the old worldly maxim:

> "There's a little bit of good in the worst of us,
> There's a little bit of bad in the best of us;
> So it little behooves the best of us
> To say anything about the worst of us."

That is a bit of sugary philosophy that would pass off with many as being charitable. The only thing is that it is worldly philosophy, totally eliminating the Cross and the complete redemption Christ offers.

Not many days after our talk, that same minister knelt with me in prayer. He had overheard some of the elders in his church arguing outside his office. Worse still, it was just before communion. Worst of all, one man used profane and sinful language. When challenged, the elder had this to say: "Our minister always taught that there is something basically incurable in man's nature; because of this, Christians must ever be willing to be the unwilling victim of uncontrollable temper and erupting hate."

That statement torpedoed the minister's theology! His elder had been a Christian of many years' standing, but he was a thorn in the flesh to many. He was patently unfruitful in his private Christian life and unprofitable to the church. He was very far removed from the apostolic standard of an elder. Under the onslaught that had flowed from the elder's abusive language, the minister's theology buckled. The main difficulty was that by his own word, the minister had acres of territory in his own life that Christ had never touched. He had a stubborn will that he excused as "knowing his own mind." (He hated that same attitude in his wife.) In him there was a deep current of bitterness that squirmed at the success of less gifted brethren in the ministry. He also found it very hard to praise others or to let another have the limelight while he stood in the shadow.

Once the illumination of the blessed Holy Spirit begins in a life, and once He is allowed to progress in His revelation of the need, there follows a terrible and humiliating heart exposure. But what good is the frightful exposure if there is no deliverance on this side of the grave from the misery and menace of sin?

Let's face it. Every religion in the world is struggling with this problem of sin. The ways that many attempt to bring peace to the penitents are weird and even wicked. The Christian alone can sing, "Blessed assurance!" The Spirit alone can bear witness that all is clear between a soul—once defiled, damned, and weighted with wickedness—and a thrice-holy God. Through the blood of His cross, Christ has made peace.

The cross itself has no power, no virtue, no deliverance. It is the blood of Jesus Christ, God's Son, that cleanseth from all sin. No amount of "stations of the cross" in a church will avail. Unless one has pleaded the merit of Christ's blood and accepted His finished work on the cross for his individual life, penances and tears, even with contrition, are valueless.

Once Dr. A. B. Simpson was preaching at a conference where different theological phrases were used for a second work of grace. The first speaker gave a drastic word on the eradication of the "old man." The second speaker spoke in a conciliatory way on suppression. Eradication, suppression—what was there left? With calm dignity, Dr. Simpson spoke on habitation: "that Christ may *dwell in your hearts* by faith." Yes, there is perfect cleansing by the blood, but there is more. Oh the glory of the indwelling Christ!

Dr. J. S. Stewart has contended that Paul's main argument is not justification or yet sanctification, but identification. Glorious thought! In this blessed oneness with Christ, there is no conflict in the will. Well has the poet put it:

> "Sweet will of God, still fold me closer
> Till I am wholly lost in Thee."

The will of God and the human will of the truly sanctified and Spirit-filled soul blend together. Like two streams flowing down a mountain side, they suddenly join together and therein forever blend as one. This is the blessedness and peace of the life that is "hid with Christ in God."

> "Thy wonderful grand will, my God,
> With triumph now I make it mine;
> And faith shall cry a joyous Yes!
> To every dear command of Thine."

The fact is that most of us believers want to run our own lives. In the Garden of Eden, Satan did not offer Eve fruit; he offered power in the words, "Ye shall be as gods." From that day to this, he has successfully dangled this offer of power before men. To another Man he once offered the kingdom of this world, but He refused them and replied, "Lo, I come to do [God's] will." Christ's fidelity to the will of His Father is shown in the bitter struggle of Gethsemane: "Nevertheless, not my will but thine be done." Let the Christian's self-will be put to death by being crucified with Christ. Then by God's given grace, let him abide in Christ. This puts a Christian on the road to victory.

Some represent the Spirit-filled life as "living underneath a cloudless sky." This phrase demands interpretation. Because Christians' experiences did not work out as cloudless as the smooth phraseology of the preacher who taught it, many have fallen back from a spiritual height and become discouraged. There may have been a glorious day when I was willing individually to accept that Christ has put to death "the old man" *for* me, and when by faith that fact became real *in* me. But to put the old man to death did not put the devil to death. He may still traffic as an angel of light or as a roaring lion. Let's settle for this: The devil is on the warpath and will keep at it "till death do us part." Only after death shall I be out of his range; though, thank God, I can be out of his power right here and now. What Satan wants is for *his* power to work through *my* powers against *God's* power. But God wants *His* power to swallow up *my* power so that "the power of Christ may rest upon me," and I may fight against principalities and powers.

To many of us the problem is not what it costs us personally to do the will of God but what it costs others when we do it. Maybe to do the will of God will mean a separation from loved ones; perhaps there will be the yielding up of a profitable career in order to fulfill a ministry in one of the forgotten holes of the earth. Maybe it will mean the postponement of marriage. Right here the enemy puts on pressure, and we recognize afresh that the Christian life is not a bed of roses but it is a warfare.

In a Christian's choices, four wills are often involved: God's will, his own will, the devil's will, and other people's wills. Sometimes other people's wills are the hardest to strive against. The Scripture has the answer: "He that doeth the will of God abideth for ever." Friends may desert or defile us. That was the way the Master went, but He triumphed. His victory is the pledge of our victory. The apostolic affirmation was that Paul could "do *all* things through Christ who strengtheneth [him]." This power was not available for Paul alone, for the Apostle was speaking to all who are cleansed, crucified, and committed.

By the crucifying of the old life, by the cleansing of the precious blood, and by the mighty indwelling of the Holy Ghost, we are to know an inner God-performed transformation. Then when self-will has been crucified, and we have been cleansed by the blood of His cross, transfiguration begins to be manifest. Up to this point all was preparatory. From here on "the beauty of the Lord our God shall be upon us." Now the unfettered soul can "mount up with wings; . . . run, and not be weary; . . . walk, and not faint."

Clarence W. Hall has written a fine life story of Samuel Logan Brengle. When speaking of the second crisis that came to Brengle, he says: "It is as though all nature, visible and invisible, had nodded its head in testifying assent, and in the next instant had begun the movement of a cool refreshing breeze within him and started springs of sparkling water bubbling up all through his being. Whereas all previous blessings have been transitory, coming and going, this experience has the 'feel' of permanency. His throat emits no shout, his feet do not dance, but his face registers unmistakably what has happened. One of the students to whom, twenty minutes after his experience, he returns a book he borrowed yesterday, looks sharply at him and asks, 'Sam, what is the matter? *You look so different!* [italics mine].' " Later, Hall says that another man, who became one of America's best-known preachers at almost the same time as the above words of a student were made, said similarly of Brengle: "Sam, I saw you about twenty feet away on the stairway, and the moment I saw you I said to myself, 'Something has happened to Brengle.' "

"By the mouth of two witnesses shall every word be established." A like experience befell the beloved principal of Cliff College, Thomas Cook, author of the popular spiritual classic *New Testament Holiness*. He was traveling on a ship for a preaching tour of South Africa. One night when the stateroom was packed with gamblers and reeking with tobacco fumes, Thomas Cook threw open the door and walked calmly through the play room. Thomas Cook said no word, just walked quietly through the den of gamblers and out at the far end of the room. Instantly men grabbed their cards and stuffed them in their pockets. Pipes were held under the tables, and a sense of awe gripped the worldly crowd. When he was gone, men asked, "Why did we do that? We never saw that done before. Why did we hide our cards?" One spoke up: "You could not do wrong in *the presence of a face like that* [italics mine]." Is this what Nietzsche was appealing for when he said, "If you want me to believe in your Redeemer, *look* more redeemed"?

I am not inferring that this endowment is a kind of perpetual nonforfeitable bonus for obedience to the will of God. Soul-calm radiating through the personality is maintained only by prayer and close submission to the will of God. In Acts 4:13 the scribes and elders took knowledge of Peter and John that they had been with Jesus.

On the Mount the immediate reaction of Peter, James, and John to the manifestation of supernatural power in Christ's transfiguration was that they fell on their faces. The Transfiguration must have been a mighty inspiration to worship! Only mute worship and prostrate adoration were fitting for such a scene. When Christ's transfiguration convinces us that we also can be transfigured, we too shall know "joy unspeakable and full of glory."

There on the Mount the disciples heard the Father's voice, and in turn heard the voices of the Son, of Moses and Elijah, and of Peter too (Mark 9:4, 5). Then in the dreadful silence of the unveiled majesty of Jesus, the order for them seemed to be "Be still and know that I am God." After our transfiguration there will also be times when Christ will be silent to us with nothing to communicate. We, too, shall be mute before Him, and beholding Him, worship.